CW00373681

THE BEST
WNES
IN THE
SUPER
MARKETS
2006

THE BEST WINES IN THE SUPER MARKETS 2006

NED HALLEY

foulsham
LONDON • NEW YORK • TORONTO • SYDNEY

foulsham

The Publishing House, Bennetts Close, Cippenham, Slough, Berkshire, SL1 5AP, England

Foulsham books can be found in all good bookshops or direct from www.foulsham.com

ISBN 0-572-03151-3

Copyright © 2006 Ned Halley

Series, format and layout design copyright © 2006 W. Foulsham & Co. Ltd

A CIP record for this book is available from the British Library

The moral right of the author has been asserted

All rights reserved

The Copyright Act prohibits (subject to certain very limited exceptions) the making of copies of any copyright work or of a substantial part of such a work, including the making of copies by photocopying or similar process. Written permission to make a copy or copies must therefore normally be obtained from the publisher in advance. It is advisable also to consult the publisher if in any doubt as to the legality of any copying which is to be undertaken.

Printed in Italy

Contents

—— *A Personal Word* ——

This is an exclusive guide. It describes the wines on sale only in that clique of retailers formed by the supermarket chains. It is in these places that we buy three-quarters of all the wine we drink at home.

Each of the big chains sells several hundred different wines, and it is by no means easy to guess what an untried bottle might taste like or whether it will turn out to be good value for money. The point of this book is to give the reader some clues.

To make it as straightforward as possible, I have divided the book up according to the supermarkets themselves. Under each name, I have arranged the recommended wines first by colour, second by price range, up to £5 and above £5, and finally by country of origin – because that's the way the supermarkets arrange the wines on their shelves.

With very few exceptions, all the wines mentioned here are recommendations. I have a simple scoring system up to 10 points to indicate quality-value ratio (see Scoring System on page 25) and anything scoring 7 or above is, I believe, worth buying at the price shown.

This is an exclusive guide in another sense. It leaves out most of the very well known brands that are available in most, if not all, supermarkets. This does not mean I do not recommend Jacob's Creek and Ernest & Julio Gallo, a couple of whose wines have made it into this edition. It just means that I am not willing to fill the following pages with their eternally repeating names.

The wines that do get mentioned are in the main less well known. Many are the own-brands of the supermarkets in question. As many as I can find are from quirky individual growers who make wine in small quantities.

Admittedly, supermarkets are not famous for stocking wines produced on a very small scale. When you have 600 branches to supply and expectations of shifting every wine in large, fast volumes, a couple of hundred cases of some rare vintage are not going to go very far. But some supermarkets do nevertheless include such wines among their faster-moving stock, and they are well worth seeking out.

Most of the wines in this book are in the price categories that account for most sales. About 88 per cent of wines sold for drinking at home cost under £5. About 18 per cent fall into the £4.50 to £6 bracket and a mere 4 per cent cost above £6.

Naturally, I believe most of the best wines are accounted for in that exclusive 4 per cent, and there are a good few of them in these pages. But the real point of this book is to recommend wines at prices that I – and you – know we're willing to pay.

The good news is that there is a lot of wine out there at affordable prices. Britain has the best choice of wine of any country in the world, and despite the monstrous taxation levied on it, it seems to me to be a luxury we can all afford – and a thoroughly healthy and civilising luxury at that.

I must apologise in advance for the inevitable fact that some of the wines I have recommended will have been discontinued or replaced with a new vintage or increased (they're never decreased) in price by the time you are reading this.

And I must reiterate the plea that what I say about the wines and the retailers is based on my personal knowledge or understanding. Taste in all things is personal, and more so than most when it comes to wine. But I hope the impressions I have given of the hundreds of wines recommended in this guide will tempt you to try some new styles and flavours, and to look beyond all those beckoning brand names to the genuine, individual wines still clinging to their shelf space.

Finding Favourites

If you have a favourite wine but don't know where it might appear in this book, check the index starting on page 189. And please note that lots of the wines I have mentioned are sold in several different supermarkets, but it's quite possible I have not included individual wines under the sections for every chain that does so. Doing this would fill the book with repetitions. But if you've seen a wine in, say, Asda, but can't find it in that section, it's still worth looking it up in the index in case I have tasted it at another supermarket and written it up under that heading.

Introduction

The supermarkets have the take-home market for wine just about completely sewn up. Nearly eight bottles out of every ten are bought from multiples and the traditional off-licence shops are having a relatively hard time of it.

I say relatively, because the wine business is booming and this means all kinds of retailers can benefit from the growth in wine drinking if they are any good. Sales of wine have increased by about 5 per cent in terms of value in the last year and are predicted to continue to grow at this sort of rate for years to come.

As the overall market expands, so does the top end. Nine out of ten bottles bought still cost under £5, but the proportion of wines costing between £4.50 and £6.00 is moving up.

And wine prices in Britain are moving up anyway. This is due partly to the slow slide of sterling against the euro – down more than 10 per cent over the last few years – but there has also been a contribution from the Chancellor of the Exchequer. Mr Brown's last three budgets have added nearly 15 pence in duty and VAT per bottle, which has further incentivised cross-Channel 'booze cruising' and made it that much harder for retailers to maintain 'price points' from the endangered £2.99 bottle upwards.

But continental Europe is no longer the prime source of our wine supplies. While once France, Italy and Spain had a near monopoly, they have faded astonishingly in recent years in the face of competition from further afield. In the last year alone, sales of Bordeaux wines in Britain have reportedly fallen by a quarter. Australia is taking up the slack, having nearly a quarter of the take-home trade. The USA and South Africa have already overtaken Italy and both of them may well push France out of second position if current trends continue. Spain is nowhere.

It's a very competitive business. Everyone wants a piece of the action, because Britain is the world's biggest importer of quality wines, and getting bigger every day. We drink about 1.2 billion bottles of wine a year – 20 bottles per head of population or, more relevantly, 40 bottles per head of the wine-drinking population (two-thirds of all adults, apparently). It sounds a lot, but it's still less per capita than other northern European countries such as the Netherlands and Denmark, and less than half the consumption in wine-producing countries including Italy and Portugal.

We have, in other words, a long way to go in terms of quantity. I hope, too, that we have a similar distance to travel in terms of quality and choice. As the British market 'matures' and more of us seek to trade up to more interesting wines, I sincerely hope the supermarkets will be there, expanding their ranges to tempt us.

——————*The Choice*——————

This book categorises the wines by nation of origin. This is largely to follow the manner in which retailers arrange their wines, but also because it is the country or region of origin that still most distinguishes one style of wine from another. True, wines are now commonly labelled most prominently with their constituent grape variety, but to classify all the world's wines into the small number of principal grape varieties would make for categories of an unwieldy size.

Chardonnay and Sauvignon Blanc are overwhelmingly dominant among whites, and four grapes – Cabernet Sauvignon, Merlot, Shiraz and Tempranillo – account for a very high proportion of red wines made worldwide.

But each area of production still – in spite of creeping globalisation – puts its own mark on its wines. Chardonnays from France remain (for the moment at least) quite distinct from those of Australia. Cabernet Sauvignon grown in a cool climate such as that of Bordeaux is a very different wine from Cabernet cultivated in the cauldron of the Barossa.

Of course there are 'styles' that winemakers worldwide seek to follow. Yellow, oaky Chardonnays of the type pioneered in South Australia are now made in South Africa, too – and in new, high-tech wineries in New Zealand and Chile, Spain and Italy. But the variety is still wide. Even though the 'upfront' high-alcohol wines of the New World have grabbed so much of the market, France continues to make the elegant wines it has always made in its classic regions. Germany still produces racy, delicate Rieslings, and the distinctive zones of Italy, Portugal and Spain make ever more characterful wines from indigenous grapes (as opposed to imported global varieties).

Among less expensive wines, the theme is, admittedly, very much a varietal one. The main selling point for most 'everyday' wines is the grape of origin rather than the country of origin. It makes sense, because the characteristics of various grape varieties do a great deal to identify taste. A bottle of white wine labelled 'Chardonnay' can reasonably be counted on to deliver that distinctive peachy or pineappley smell and soft, unctuous apple flavours. A Sauvignon Blanc should evoke gooseberries, green fruit and grassy freshness. And so on.

For all the domination of Chardonnay and Cabernet, there are plenty of other grape varieties making their presence felt. Argentina, for example, has revived the fortunes of several French and Italian varieties that had become near-extinct at home. And the grape that (in my view) can make the most exciting of white wines, the Riesling, is now doing great things in the southern hemisphere as well as at home in Germany.

Among the current market trends, most notable is the rise of rosé wine. The trade is putting it down to the blistering summer of 2003, during which red wine sales suffered, but pink wines more than made up for the loss. Despite two rather mixed summers in the intervening years, sales of rosé have continued to soar, and now stand at nearly double the level of 2000.

—Can you Spot the—
Grape Variety?

The character of most wines is defined largely by the grape variety, and it is a source of innocent pleasure to be able to identify which variety it is without peeking at the label. Here are some of the characteristics to look for in wines from the ten most widely used varieties.

White

Chardonnay: Colour from pale to straw gold. Aroma can evoke peach, pineapple, sweet apple. Flavours of sweet apple, with creaminess or toffee from oak contact.

Riesling: In German wines, pale colour, sharp-apple aroma, racy fruit whether dry or sweet. Faint spritz common in young wines. Petrolly hint in older wines.

Sauvignon Blanc: Pale colour with suggestion of green. Aromas of asparagus, gooseberries, nettles. Green, grassy fruit.

Semillon: Colour can be rich yellow. Aromas of tropical fruit including pineapple and bananas. Even in dry wines, hints of honey amid fresh, fruit-salad flavours.

Viognier: Intense pale-gold colour. Aroma evokes apricots, blanched almonds and fruit blossom. Flavours include candied fruits. Finish often low in acidity.

Red

Cabernet Sauvignon: Dense colour, purple in youth. Strong aroma of blackcurrants and cedar wood ('cigar box'). Flavour concentrated, often edged with tannin so it grips the mouth.

Merlot: Dark, rich colour. Aroma of sweet black cherry. Plummy, rich, mellow fruit can be akin to Cabernet but with less tannin. May be hints of bitter chocolate.

Pinot Noir: Colour distinctly pale, browning with age. Aromas of strawberry and raspberry. Light-bodied wine with soft-fruit flavours but dry, clean finish.

Shiraz: Intense, near-black colour. Aroma of ripe fruit, sometimes spicy. Robust, rich flavours, commonly with high alcohol, but with soft tannins.

Tempranillo: Colour can be pale, as in Rioja. Blackcurrant aroma, often accompanied by vanilla from oak ageing. Tobacco, even leather, evoked in flavours.

There is more about all these varieties, and many others, in 'What Wine Words Mean' starting on page 127.

—Fizz Market Sparkles—

The sparkling wine business is booming, with Champagne leading the way. Britain is by a mile the biggest importer of Champagne in the world. In 2004 we set a new record of 35 million bottles, and got through about the same quantity of 'alternative' fizzes, ranging from inexpensive sweet Asti Spumante to the much costlier sparklers now made in Australia and New Zealand, California and Latin America – and even in England and Wales.

When shopping for sparkling wine, it's a reliable rule that you get what you pay for. Champagne is notoriously expensive, especially here in Britain, where the highest prices in the world maintain the wine's luxury image and pay for the upmarket promotions that perpetuate the notion of the 'Champagne lifestyle'.

In fairness to the Champagne industry, their product is nevertheless one of life's most exciting, and accessible, special treats. Compared to the price of tickets to a Premiership football match or a night in a decent hotel, the £20 or £25 you pay for a famous Champagne such as Moët & Chandon or Veuve Clicquot looks like peanuts.

The ceremony of opening a bottle of Champagne is an occasion in its own right. The wine needs to be chilled, but not freezing. An hour in the fridge will do the trick or, in an emergency, 15 minutes in the freezer. Tulip-shaped wine glasses are fine if you don't have the narrow Champagne 'flutes' that long ago displaced the saucer-shaped glass.

There's a trick to opening a Champagne bottle without fuss. First, avoid shaking the bottle beforehand. Unless you're celebrating a Grand Prix victory, it's a tragic waste of the wine to have it frothing into the carpet rather than gliding into the glass.

Once you've stripped off the foil and the wire cage, grip the cork with one hand, and the body of the bottle with the other. Turn the bottle, not the cork, and keep a hold of the cork as it eases out. It should emerge with a sigh, rather than a bang.

Into each glass, pour just a centimetre of wine, then move on to the next glass. When you return to fill the glasses, this prevents the wine fizzing wildly up in the glass and overflowing.

The French, who drink five times as much Champagne as we do, are very keen on serving it with food. It's not – yet, anyway – the convention here, but it is a great treat to have a glass of fizz with oysters, smoked salmon and other fishy delights. And there is a long tradition of serving it with foie gras. 'My idea of heaven,' said Sydney Smith 200 years ago, 'is eating pâté de foie gras and drinking Champagne to the sound of trumpets.'

────────The Price ────────

How do retailers price their wines? Some bottles do seem inexplicably cheap, others unjustifiably expensive. But there is often a simple explanation. Big retailers work to price points. In wine, these are £2.99, £3.49, £3.99, even £9.99. You'll find very few bottles priced anywhere between these 50p spacings. A wine that wouldn't be profitable at £4.99 but would be at, say, £5.11, is priced at £5.49 in the hope that shoppers won't be wise to the fact that it is relatively poor value.

It's true that there are some wines on supermarket shelves priced at £3.29, £3.79, etc. And 2005 has yet again seen many retailers attempt to pass the third successive 4p Budget rise in excise duty directly on to the customer, only to allow the price to subside back to the .99 point. But at whose expense? It tends to be the supplier, rather than the retailer.

But price can be a poor guide to quality even at the best of times. The only means by which any of us can determine a wine's value is by personal taste. The ideal bottle is one you like very much and would buy again at the same price without demur.

Just for curiosity's sake, though, it's fun to know what the wine itself actually costs, and what the retailer is making on it. The table overleaf shows how the costs break down in a French wine costing £4.49 at a supermarket. This is a slightly unusual purchase by a supermarket, because the wine is being bought direct from the vineyard where it was made. Usually, retail multiples buy their wines by a less strenuous method, from agents and distributors in the UK.

Price paid by supermarket to supplier in	
France for the bottled wine	£1.40
Transport and insurance to UK	£0.27
Excise duty	£1.27
Cost to supermarket	£2.94
Supermarket's routine mark-up at 30%	£0.88
VAT at 17.5% on marked-up price	£0.67
Shelf price in supermarket	£4.49

The largest share of the money appears to go to the producer in France. But from his £1.40 he must pay the cost of growing and harvesting the grapes, pressing them, fermenting the juice, clarifying and treating the wine. Then he must bottle, cork, encapsulate, label and pack the wine into cartons. If his margin after these direct costs is 50p, he's doing well.

The prime profiteer, however, is not the supermarket, even though it makes a healthy 88p in mark-up. It is the Chancellor who does best, by miles. Excise duty and VAT are two of the cheapest taxes to collect and from this single bottle of wine, the Treasury trousers a princely £1.94.

Travellers to wine-producing countries are always thrilled to find that by taking their own bottles, jugs or plastic casks to rustic vineyards offering wine on tap they can buy drinkable stuff for as little as 50p a litre. What too few travellers appreciate is that, for the wine itself, that's about what the supermarkets are paying for it. When enjoying your bargain bottle of wine, it is interesting to reflect on the economic reality known as 'added value' – which dictates that the worthiest person in the chain, the producer, has probably earned less than 10 per cent of the final price.

—A Matter of Closures—

Every year, the number of wines 'closed' by methods other than the traditional cork grows. Thanks to a widespread belief that the quality of natural corks has long been in decline, ruining many otherwise perfectly good bottles of wine, alternative 'closures' have become something of a holy grail.

Some supermarkets, notably Tesco, are determinedly weeding out the traditional cork, and insisting that their suppliers bottle with plastic bungs or metal screwcaps. And there are plenty of producers, in Europe (where the corks come from) as well as in the New World, who are quite happy to dispense with this old technology – which dates back to the eighteenth century.

But there are two sides to the story, and since I made a visit to the cork forests of Portugal, I've been trying to take a balanced view, especially as the debate has lately become rather heated.

On the very morning I set out for Portugal, an announcement arrived in the post from a top New Zealand wine company. It was headlined: 'Villa Maria Says Screw Corks'.

Villa Maria's owner, George Fistonich, is refusing to sell any more wine in bottles with corks. 'We are 100 per cent committed to the quality that the use of screwcap closures guarantees,' he declares. 'To achieve this, Villa Maria has had to inform distributors that it is screwcaps or nothing. This may seem a little harsh, but no other industry in the world accepts the type of product failure experienced using cork.'

Reading this at the airport, waiting for the plane to Lisbon, I began to wonder if Mr Fistonich might be objecting just a little too much. True, we have all heard of 'corked' wine, but after centuries of happily confining wine in bottles with nothing else, is the cork really dead?

There are plenty of winemakers, and retailers, who think so. One in ten bottles now has either a plastic stopper or a screwcap. It's due to a recent surge in the number of wines spoiled by a taint known as 2,4,6-trichloroanisole, or TCA, which imparts an unpleasant, musty aroma and flavour – and has been blamed roundly on the cork manufacturers.

And so to Portugal, where the country's – and the world's – biggest cork producer, Amorim, invited me to see for myself what is being done about it.

I am met by Carlos de Jesus, Amorim's marketing director, who conducts me to the cork oak forests, starting an hour's drive north-east of Lisbon and extending over hundreds of square miles beyond. It's the harvest, and highly skilled men armed with light, broad-bladed axes are stripping the trunks and lower branches of the trees of their bark, up to three inches thick, in sections several feet long. The process takes place once every nine years.

'It's like a face peel in beauty treatment,' says Carlos. 'It leaves the skin a little tender, but renewed. We harvest between May and August, when growth is at its most active. The first harvest is after 25 years. It does the trees no harm. They live up to 200 years.'

This is obviously the most natural and renewable means of providing the raw material for bottle stoppers. And I do wonder how the wine industry could ever have adopted cork-shaped stoppers made from what Carlos likes to call 'oil-derived products' instead.

But plastic 'corks' look doomed. They can be difficult to extract and hard to unwind from the corkscrew afterwards. It's impossible to push them back into the bottle. They utterly lack the indispensable elasticity of natural cork.

It is the screwcap that is the only real long-term rival for cork. It obviates the corkscrew, and may, in time, prove to be as good at preserving the wine in healthy condition, as well as being proof against tainted flavour.

Back in the forest, we next visit a huge Amorim plant where the peeled bark is stacked in endless canyons, several metres high, before being boiled in newly installed vats incorporating a continuous water-filtering system to remove impurities and combat the dreaded taint.

'In the last two and a half years we have spent 43 million dollars on re-equipping to fight TCA,' says Carlos. It's a candid admission that the infection has indeed been a problem for this major industry, employing 20,000 people in Portugal.

Extensive research suggests that the taint has become more common due to chemical reactions with chlorine products used in the wine industry. But Carlos is quick to point out that TCA does not affect only cork. 'It can adhere to wood, to concrete, to metal and to plastic – including oil-derived stoppers and screwcaps too,' he says, reminding us of the winery in the US that lately traced the TCA in its wine to an infection not in its corks but in its drainage system. The infection was so severe the entire plant had to be closed down.

The task at Amorim is to ensure that all the three billion corks they produce annually are TCA free. And they are succeeding. In the last year, sales of their Twin Top cork, formed by a disc of whole cork at either end of a cylinder of agglomerated cork granules, have passed 800 million – and there has been a complaint about only one of them.

It's down to changed practices in the company's dozen production centres, including a new steam-treatment system, specifically developed to counter TCA, through which every single cork passes. The company has also installed gas chromatography equipment to detect any infections.

I was greatly impressed with what Amorim have achieved, and as the world's biggest manufacturer, the company is doing great things to restore the good name of their own corks, if not the many more that are made by other producers in Portugal, Spain and around the world.

But can Amorim hope that these heroic efforts will impress winemakers such as George Fistonich?

Antonio Amorim, chairman of the 134-year-old company, acknowledges that views have become polarised. 'In Europe cork and wine is an old marriage. It's accepted,' he told me. 'But in the New World they question everything and I don't blame them for that.'

He acknowledges that his own industry was slow to respond to the TCA crisis in the 1990s, as the wine trade started to blame every duff bottle on TCA-affected corks, even though cork was really only responsible for a fraction of the total.

'Six or seven years ago in this industry we could only talk philosophy, but now we can talk science,' he said. 'TCA is a problem we feel we have solved, although I would never claim to have eradicated it. But now we can start to speak about the many positive aspects of cork, how it contributes to the good of wine, to its health and development.'

He seems calmly confident, and is prepared for a long campaign of championing the cork. 'We are patient people,' he says. 'After all, we wait 25 years to collect our first harvest, and we are prepared to take time to convince consumers that this natural product is the best one for now and for the future.'

—The Supermarket—
Best Wine Buys

First, a short explanation of my scoring system. As an entirely subjective guide to relative value among the wines mentioned in the book, I use a scoring scale of 0 to 10. In the notes I took while tasting, I gave each wine a score within this range, and just about all the wines that were given a score of 7 and above are included. Wines scoring 6 and under are all left out, because this is not a book in which there is space to decry wines I have not liked.

I would recommend any of the wines with a score of 7 or above. Those scoring 7 are those I account good wines at a fair price. A score of 8 signifies a very good wine at a fair price and a score of 9 indicates special quality and value. Those that earn 10 out of 10 are, obviously enough, the wines I don't think can be bettered.

Out of the hundreds I have tasted, just 25 wines scored the maximum 10 out of 10 on my personal scale. They are listed overleaf. A good number of them are very inexpensive and are rated so highly because they seemed to me quite remarkable value for money. If it really signifies anything, it might be of interest to point out that the number of top scores was highest from Waitrose, with nine, followed by four from Majestic, Booths and Marks & Spencer, two from Sainsbury's and one apiece for the rest. Countries of origin are led by France with eight top scores, three for Australia, New Zealand and Spain, two apiece for Argentina, Germany and Italy and one each for Chile and South Africa.

My Top Supermarket Wines

Red Wines

£5.49	Arrogant Frog Ribet Red Vin de Pays d'Oc 2003	France	Booths
£6.99	Chianti Burchino 2003	Italy	Marks & Spencer
£9.99	Côtes de Nuits Villages 2002	France	Marks & Spencer
£5.97	Evans & Tate Classic Red 2003	Australia	Asda
£12.99	Givry 1er Cru Vieilles Vignes, Domaine Sarrazin, 2003	France	Majestic
£3.49	Sainsbury's Argentinian Bonarda NV	Argentina	Sainsbury
£8.49	Sainsbury's Classic Selection Rioja Reserva Elegia 1999	Spain	Sainsbury
£7.55	Saumur-Champigny Les Tuffeaux, Château de Targé, 2003	France	Majestic and Waitrose
£4.55	Saumur Les Nivières 2003	France	Waitrose
£7.99	Stoneleigh Pinot Noir 2003	New Zealand	Waitrose
£13.99	Vergelegen Cabernet Sauvignon 2001	South Africa	Majestic
£2.99	Vina Decana Crianza 2000	Spain	Aldi
£9.99	Vino Nobile di Montepulciano, Carbonaia, 2001	Italy	Waitrose

White Wines

£9.99	Catena Chardonnay 2003	Argentina	Waitrose
£9.99	Ernst Loosen Erdener Treppchen Riesling Kabinett 2004	Germany	Marks & Spencer
£9.95	Hattenheimer Wisselbrunnen Riesling Spätlese, Von Simmern, 2002	Germany	Waitrose
£7.99	Hermit Crab Marsanne Viognier, D'Arenberg Vineyards, 2003	Australia	Booths
£7.99	Kaituna Hills Reserve Sauvignon Blanc 2004	New Zealand	Marks & Spencer
£5.99	St Hallet Poacher's Blend 2004	Australia	Co-op
£7.49	Tesco Finest Marlborough Sauvignon Blanc 2004	New Zealand	Tesco

Rosé Wine

£5.49	Torres San Medin Cabernet Sauvignon Rosé 2004	Chile	Booths and Waitrose

Sparkling Wines

£12.99	Champagne Baron-Fuenté Brut	France	Booths
£35.99	Champagne Perrier-Jouët Brut 1998	France	Majestic
£19.99	Waitrose Brut Vintage Champagne 1996	France	Waitrose

Fortified Wine

£6.55	Waitrose Solera Jerezano Dry Amontillado Sherry	Spain	Waitrose

Aldi

This German 'no-frills' chain has 5,000 supermarkets across Europe, including 250 in the UK. The stores are already a genuine source of wine bargains, and the company is setting about improving and extending the range.

It's worth keeping an eye on the stores for occasional bargain-priced classed-growth clarets of really astounding quality, but these do tend to sell out rather fast. Steadier lines include some remarkable buys, such as drinkable mature Bordeaux at £2.99 and Languedoc wines from one of France's most-praised producers, Jean-Paul Mas.

If you don't know where your nearest Aldi is, ring the Store Location Line on 08705 134262 or look on the net at **www.aldi-stores.co.uk**.

FRANCE

🍷 9 Château Selection Claret 2001   £2.99
Impressively dense colour and flavour to this ridiculously
cheap Bordeaux with soft, ripe mature fruit.

🍷 8 Château Les Lesques,
Charles de Monteney, 2002   £3.29
Dark colour and slightly austere edge to the blackcurrant
fruit in this quite-gripping Bordeaux at a very low price.

🍷 9 Ile La Forge Merlot 2003   £4.99
Bumper vin de pays d'Oc is black in both colour and
flavour, especially in the cherry-and-chocolate middle
fruit. Big wine with 14% alcohol to relish with
assertively flavoured meat dishes. Very smart packaging
belies the bargain price.

🍷 8 Ile La Forge Syrah 2003   £4.99
Vividly brambly and spicy Languedoc food wine.

ITALY

🍷 9 Casa Laora Chianti 2003   £3.49
Pale but very interesting dry cherry and plum fruit
Chianti of entirely authentic quality in spite of such a low
price. True bargain.

SPAIN

🍷 10 Vina Decana Crianza 2000   £2.99
Bright and crisply clean mature wine with squishy red-
fruit flavours and a good edge of acidity. This is
delightful glugging Spanish red of real interest, and at a
price I find completely inexplicable!

RED WINES   £5 PLUS

FRANCE

 8 **Château du Moulin Rouge 2001**   £7.99
Aldi periodically offer classed-growth claret at rock-bottom prices, and this Haut Médoc cru bourgeois is another excellent one, with intense, gripping dark fruit in the proper minty-silky style. Best from 2007.

PINK WINES   UNDER £5

SPAIN

8 **Vina Decana Rosado 2004**   £2.99
Bright magenta colour, cherry-drop nose and a lively strawberry fruit with caramel background make this all rather fun.

WHITE WINES   UNDER £5

FRANCE

8 **Charles de Monteney Chardonnay 2003**   £3.29
Nutty, buttery scent to this gently ripe Midi white is
followed up by soft but balanced fruit, finishing clean.

8 **Ile La Forge Chardonnay 2004**   £4.99
Clean, brisk dry white fermented in oak, but by no means
overwhelmed by the wood. Nice balance.

ITALY

8 **Villa Malizia Pinot Grigio 2004**   £3.99
Zesty variation on the unstoppable PG theme has a nice
smoky back flavour, moderated sweetness and as much
interest as other, more expensive PGs of my
acquaintance.

SPAIN

8 **Vina Decana Bianco 2004**   £2.99
Softly appealing dry white with balancing crispness is
easy drinking.

Asda

Originally formed by a group of farmers seeking a steady outlet for their products – the name is simply a contraction of Associated Dairies – Asda has long since grown into a giant. Now part of US retail behemoth Wal-Mart, it has done well to retain its friendly image. Its stores are invariably vast, and yet contrive, in my experience at least, to be unreservedly welcoming.

Wine is probably not among the primary attractions of Asda, but I am glad to say that, after recent improvements in the chain's range, it deserves to be. Although still dominated by the same 'global brands' that crowd the shelves of its direct competitors, Asda is sneaking in some very nifty individual wines, and improving its own-label selection enormously.

Price promotions, as might be expected, are a regular feature. And as a permanent attraction, if you buy any six bottles of wine, you get 10 per cent off the lot. As far as I know, no other supermarket offers this – it's 5 per cent at the other Big Three chains.

Most of the wines commended here are from Australia and Spain, as these have comprised the majority of those offered for tasting this year. I am assured, however, that Asda do have wines from other countries too.

RED WINES   UNDER £5

9 **Angove's Bear Crossing Cabernet
Shiraz 3-litre box**   **£12.98**

AUSTRALIA

Dense and meaty red with 14% alcohol, but also healthily juicy with squishy blackberry fruit. Quality is way above average for bag-in-box wine at a price equivalent to £3.25 a bottle.

9 **Asda Australian Reserve Shiraz 2003**   **£4.98**
Bright, purple colour, new-crushed berry fleshiness of flavour and a sinful streak of vanilla in the fruit. Bargain.

8 **Viña Albali Reserva 2000**   **£4.48**
Ubiquitous La Mancha oaked red has the browning hue of maturity, beguiling sweet vanilla nose, and a hint of spiritiness.

SPAIN

9 **Vega Barcelona 2003**   **£4.98**
Gripping but not tough, this big, lush Catalonian has stacks of red-berry fruit and 13.5% alcohol.

RED WINES   £5 PLUS

9 **Evans & Tate Langhorne Creek
Shiraz 2003**   **£5.48**

AUSTRALIA

Garish colour but ultra-smooth texture to this black-fruit monster (14.5% alcohol) with vigorous, stimulating flavours.

8 **Rock Red Shiraz-Grenache-Pinot 2003**   **£5.92**
Summer-pudding fruit here, with suggestions of blackcurrants, cherries, cream and even chocolate in the flavour, and 14.5% alcohol.

RED WINES   £5 PLUS

AUSTRALIA

10 Evans & Tate Classic Red 2003   £5.97
Huge darkly toothsome fruit (14.5% alcohol) in this no-
nonsense Shiraz-Cabernet blend is simply perfect, with
positively elegant clean finish. Best Aussie red at this
price I've found all year. Screwcap.

8 Penmara Five Families Pinot Noir 2002   £5.98
Typical light bricky-red colour of Pinot Noir, and a
warmly delicious, summer-fruit wine of real character.

8 Lizards of Oz Reserve Malbec 2002   £6.98
Annoying name but a deliciously gripping black-fruit
wine with 14% alcohol, a bitter chocolate centre and a
notion of liquorice in there too.

FRANCE

8 Gérard Bertrand Pinot Noir 2001   £6.48
Summer-fruit fleshiness to this darker-than-usual
Languedoc Pinot has a trace of sunburn and plenty of
character.

8 Blason de Bourgogne Mercurey 2002   £9.98
Pale but handsome ruby colour and an intriguing
peppery nose in this healthy, strawberry-fruit burgundy
with clean, lipsmacking finish

SOUTH AFRICA

9 Diemersfontein Pinotage 2004   £6.98
Dense purple colour and an aroma of hot toast and jam
both correspond to rich, comforting flavour with
plummy depths. Fascinating food wine.

RED WINES   £5 PLUS

SPAIN

▼8   **Penedes Lignum Negre 2003**   £6.98
Dark purply colour in this smoothly oaked but vigorously blackcurranty blend from famed organic producer Albet I Noya.

▼9   **Fagus 2002**   £12.98
Chi-chi Aragon wine from pure Garnacha is dark, silky and lush with minty ripeness. Price is justified for exceptional character.

PINK WINES   UNDER £5

FRANCE

▼8   **Asda Rosé d'Anjou NV**   £2.81
Pale but cheerfully shocking pink, dry but softly fruity with strawberry ripeness, and a genuine bargain.

PINK WINES   £5 PLUS

USA

▼8   **Fetzer Valley Oaks Syrah Rosé 2004**   £5.98
Colour and aroma seem nearer red than pink, but this distinctive Californian delivers juiciness and refreshment.

WHITE WINES   UNDER £5

AUSTRALIA

▼9   **Brown Brothers Dry Muscat 2004**   £4.97
It's certainly dry, but nevertheless emphatically grapey, with a nice 'attack' of fruit in the first flavour. Very good aperitif wine. Screwcap.

CHILE

▼8   **Asda Chilean Chardonnay 2004**   £2.97
Ridiculously cheap for this sort of tangy, lively quality. Nice grapefruit style.

WHITE WINES	UNDER £5

ENGLAND

8 Asda English Regional Wine 2004   £4.78
Elderflower and grapefruit are clearly evoked in this interesting dry but not austere white by Three Choirs vineyard in Gloucestershire.

9 Three Choirs Variation Aromatic 2004   £4.98
From Gloucestershire, a shining example of how good English wine can be. It's dry, with a crisp-apple fruitiness and a touch of pastry sweetness in the aroma and flavour. Deliciously sunny.

ITALY

8 Asda Pinot Grigio del Trentino 2004   £4.98
Nice example of this fashionable item has a grassy-fresh aroma with what I thought might be a hint of greengage and a corresponding splash of zesty, green-fruit flavour.

SPAIN

8 Santerra Dry Muscat 2004 3-litre box   £12.98
Dry but grapy and unexpectedly delicious summer-party wine really tastes more like grape juice than wine, but 12% alcohol. Price is equivalent to £3.25 a bottle.

WHITE WINES	£5 PLUS

AUSTRALIA

8 Zilzie Estate Chardonnay 2004   £5.98
Richly coloured, lush with sweet-apple fruit and yet brightly fresh.

9 Jacob's Creek Reserve Chardonnay 2003   £7.99
There's no getting away from it. This is a big brand name, perhaps the biggest, but it is fabulous wine, a masterly marriage of luxury fruit with mineral, citrus acidity. Tastes like a very expensive wine indeed.

WHITE WINES   £5 PLUS

AUSTRALIA

🍷**8** **Hanging Rock Jim Jim Sauvignon
Blanc 2004**   **£11.98**
In aroma and flavour, this luxury wine is beautifully balanced between sweetness and tartness, lush, grassy and long. Exceptional, if not cheap.

FRANCE

🍷**8** **Asda Extra Special Chablis
Premier Cru 2002**   **£10.57**
Rich style of Chablis with elusive flintiness is worthy of the famous namc, and satisfyingly complex. Annoying plastic 'cork'.

NEW ZEALAND

🍷**9** **Asda New Zealand Sauvignon Blanc 2005**   **£5.48**
Nice nettley scent on this bargain wine is followed up by asparagus fruit and plenty of zest. Screwcap.

🍷**9** **Asda Extra Special New Zealand
Sauvignon Blanc 2005**   **£6.98**
Worth the price hike, this has a generous gooseberry nose, concentration of grassy fruit and a long finish.

SPARKLING WINES   £5 PLUS

AUSTRALIA

🍷**8** **Jacob's Creek Sparkling Rosé**   **£7.99**
Magenta colour, persistent mousse and a crunchy blackberry style with a trace of toffee make for an irresistible whole.

Booths

 If you are not familiar with Lancashire, you might well be unfamiliar with Booths. It's a chain of just 25 supermarkets based in the region. But its reputation for wine is nationwide. The company has an excellent website at **www.booths-wine.co.uk** or you can telephone for a mail order list, and to place orders, on 0800 197 0066. The chain also has a remarkable online operation offering more than 23,000 different wines with the apposite website name of **www.everywine.co.uk**.

RED WINES   UNDER £5

FRANCE

8 **Château Le Pin 2003** £4.99
There is another Château Le Pin in Bordeaux, which makes the world's most expensive wine. This one is therefore good for a giggle, and delicious, too – dark, vigorous, sappy, and 14% alcohol.

9 **Coteaux de Languedoc Les Ruffes
La Sauvageonne 2003** £4.99
Core of red fruit and spice in this meaty Midi mix of many grape varities. Winter stew matcher.

ITALY

8 **Barocco Rosso del Salento 2003** £3.49
Breezy lightweight red-berry vino from Italy's south is a gluggable bargain.

8 **Rapido Rosso Beneventano 2004** £3.99
Brambly but gripping dark-fruit pasta-matcher from the wonderful Campania region has a clean, dry finish.

8 **Inycon Nero d'Avola 2003** £4.99
Dark, coaly Sicilian red has a mysterious but likeable volcanic whiff about it.

SPAIN

8 **Casa Morena Bodega Felix Solis NV** £2.99
Earthy, dare I say farmyardy, style to this brisk, briary, clean-tasting thoroughly Spanish plonk.

RED WINES   £5 PLUS

ARGENTINA

8   **Alamos Bonarda 2003**   **£5.99**
Juicy, friendly Mendoza red with 13.5% alcohol and good intensity of blackcurrant fruit.

AUSTRALIA

8   **Peter Lehmann Clancy's Red 2002**   **£6.99**
Dark, baked flavour and well-judged weight to this meaty blend from Shiraz, Cabernet and Merlot with spice and Victoria plums in the mix.

8   **Ninth Island Pinot Noir 2003**   **£8.99**
Tasmanian cherry-strawberry wine has pure-fruit, natural vigour. Real quality summer red.

CHILE

9   **Casillero del Diablo**
Cabernet Sauvignon 2004   **£5.49**
Firm, blackcurranty Cabernet has generous weight, oaky velvet and stirring hint of spice. Seems cheap.

8   **Carmen Reserve Carmenère**
Cabernet Sauvignon 2002   **£8.99**
Silky minty blend with creamy oak element is extravagant but not overdone.

8   **Casa Lapostolle Cuvée Alexandre**
Merlot 2002   **£12.99**
Chile doesn't do much wine at this elevated level, but this one is a good flag-flyer. Colour is still a bit raw, but the nose and fruit are coming on nicely, showing intense concentration and ripeness (14.5% alcohol) but elegant restraint. Keep it a couple more years for a real treat.

10 **Arrogant Frog Ribet Red**
Vin de Pays d'Oc 2003   £5.49
Fantastic wine at this price is strong, structured, lipsmackingly lasting and combines the elegant, smooth Bordeaux style (it's from Cabernet and Merlot grapes) with the rugged spiciness and grip of the deep south. The jokey name might seem iffy, but the wine is faultless.

8 **Chinon Cuvée de Pâcques Domaine de**
la Roche Honneur 2003   £5.49
Purply young-tasting juicy redcurranty dry-finishing Loire Valley red of classic character.

9 **Domaine Chaume-Arnaud Côtes du Rhône**
Villages Vinsobres 2002   £7.99
Plump, roundly mature and beguiling red of unusually mellow character from the roasting Rhône is very delicious.

8 **English Oak Minervois La Livinière 2002**   £8.99
Here's a wine with bark and bite. Fetching label features an oak tree, and the wine is a Syrah-based spicy monster with plenty of rich blackberry fruit.

9 **Rasteau Prestige Domaine des Coteaux**
de Travers 2003   £8.99
Top Rhône village red has clinging spicy fruit of great appeal and 14.5% alcohol. Drink this with starchy items such as cassoulet.

8 **Château Jupille-Carillon 1999**   £9.99
Gamey St-Emilion with the cedar-wood or 'cigar-box' aroma of proper claret is nicely rounded out and elegantly balanced. Old-fashioned and virtuous.

FRANCE

RED WINES   £5 PLUS

ITALY

9 **Rosso di Montepulciano Azienda**
Agricola Poliziano 2003   £7.99
Classic darkly spicy and sleek Sangiovese red with silky
oak influence is a bargain by the standards of the
hilltown denomination of Montepulciano in Tuscany.
Lovely stuff.

9 **Barbera d'Asti Superiore La Luna e**
I Falo Terre da Vino 2002   £8.99
Unfathomable name, and the wine is pretty enigmatic
too. A luxury variation on the more everyday blueberry-
pie theme of Piedmont Barbera is vigorously fruity and
richly plush at the same time.

9 **Quintus Amarone della Valpolicella**
Cantina Valpantena 2001   £14.99
After-dinner red from sun-dried grapes is rich but not
heavy (14.5% alcohol) with dark, roasted fruit finishing
with a relishable bitter twang. Grand with cheese.

NEW ZEALAND

9 **Wither Hills Pinot Noir 2003**   £13.99
Probably the best Kiwi Pinot I've tasted in the year, but
rather expensive. Pure silk, with textbook New Zealand
minty-slinkiness and an awesome complexity. Screwcap.

PORTUGAL

9 **Grand'Arte Trincadeira DFJ Vinhos 2003** £6.99
Very dense purple-black colour to this spicy, eucalyptus-
infused black-fruit Ribatejo red. Distinctive and
thoroughly Portuguese.

RED WINES £5 PLUS

SPAIN

8 **Escobera Jumilla 2002** £5.49
Dense, minty, squishy black fruit wine has an easy balance between ripeness (13.5% alcohol) and dryness.

8 **Rioja Crianza Bodega Amezola de la Mora 2001** £8.69
No mistaking the vanilla nose on this classic Rioja, and there's lots of blackcurrant and cream style to the long, lingering fruit. Mature, but lively.

PINK WINES UNDER £5

FRANCE

8 **Domaine de Pellehaut Rosé 2004** £4.49
Strong pink colour to this Gascon vin de pays with hedgerow fruit, grip of tannin and crisp finish. Screwcap.

HUNGARY

9 **Nagyréde Estate Cabernet Rosé 2004** £3.79
Onion skin colour and a brisk cassis fruitiness to a genuinely enjoyable wine at a giveaway price.

PINK WINES £5 PLUS

CHILE

10 **Torres San Medin Cabernet Sauvignon Rosé 2004** £5.49
My top rosé of the year, and a bargain at this price. Bright, shocking pink colour, lush cassis nose and pure, crisp, lasting fruit flavours and 13.8% alcohol.

WHITE WINES	UNDER £5

FRANCE

8 **Les Deux Colombard Chardonnay 2004** £3.29
Tangy green-fruit Gascon vin de pays is brisk and refreshing. Screwcap.

8 **Château de Béranger Picpoul de Pinet 2004** £4.29
Hints of tropical fruit in this interesting dry white Hérault wine with almondy richness.

ITALY

8 **Inycon Fiano 2004** £4.99
Fiano is a grape variety dating back to ancient Rome. Today it makes oxidised, sherry-like whites, of which this Sicilian version is a delicious example.

PORTUGAL

8 **Quinta de Azevedo Vinho Verde 2004** £4.99
Very dry, almost austere, example of Portugal's once-bestselling 'green wine' is a real refresher.

SPAIN

8 **Castillo de Almansa Coleccion Blanca, Bodegas Piqueras 2004** £3.99
Crisp brassica fruit in this bracing dry white wine to drink with fish.

8 **Palacio de Bornas 2004** £4.99
Sweet spicy nose and grassy green fruit in this highly distinctive dry white from the Rueda region.

WHITE WINES	£5 PLUS

AUSTRALIA

 Brown Brothers Limited Release Riesling 1999 £5.99

Limey, bracing style to this mature but very lively aromatic dry white. Drink with tapas, smoked meats or similar.

 Hermit Crab Marsanne Viognier, D'Arenberg Vineyards, 2003 £7.99

This will bring you out of your shell! Hugely concentrated and weighty gold-coloured exotic dry white with orchard fruit and sherry notes. A real attention-grabber, with a mind-concentrating 14.5% alcohol.

CHILE

Trio Sauvignon Blanc, Concha y Toro, 2004 £5.99

Lemon-grass aroma and long, green flavours on this artful dry white.

ENGLAND

Chapel Down Bacchus 2004 £5.99

Decent aromatic dry white from Tenterden in Kent. The Bacchus grape is related to the noble Riesling.

FRANCE

 Sweet Chestnut Chardonnay 2002 £8.99

The wine is from Limoux in SW France, but the chestnut tree on the label is from Richmond Park in SW London. Nice rich dry wine of interest.

 Alsace Riesling Grand Cru Ollwiller, Cave de Turckheim 2002 £9.99

Rare wine with a beautiful sweet-apple aroma and lush, intoxicating ripe flavours.

WHITE WINES	£5 PLUS

FRANCE

9 **Chablis Premier Cru Les Lys,**
Daniel Defaix, 1998 £15.99
Daniel Defaix specialises in Chablis for long keeping, and this one is a gem, combining the flinty style of the appellation with the richness of the oaked Burgundy style.

GERMANY

8 **Riesling Kabinett Joseph Leitz 2003** £7.49
Apple blossom nose and soft but keen Riesling fruit in this Rheingau wine, with 11% alcohol.

ITALY

8 **Selva d'Oro Falchini 2004** £5.29
Floral aroma and exotic dry herbaceous flavours in this old-fashioned Tuscan white.

8 **Gavi Masseria dei Carmelitani 2004** £7.99
Aromatic Piedmontese white has elusive diesel element to its spicy dry character.

NEW ZEALAND

8 **Mud House Sauvignon Blanc 2004** £7.99
Grassy whiff and intriguing asparagus fruit in this crisp and lively Kiwi refresher. Screwcap.

SOUTH AFRICA

9 **Steenberg Semillon 2003** £7.99
Gold colour, pineapple nose, tropical fruit salad flavours and a long, lavish aftertaste to this superb Cape dry white.

SPARKLING WINES	UNDER £5

ITALY

🍷9 **Nivole Moscato d'Asti, Michele Chiarlo, 2004** **£4.99 half bottle**

Gorgeous honeyed but briskly fresh sparkler finishing wonderfully crisp and clean. Alchemic contrivance elegantly presented in a dinky slim bottle with a pull cork.

SPARKLING WINES	£5 PLUS

FRANCE

🍷10 **Champagne Baron-Fuenté Brut** **£12.99**

Encouraging gold colour, sweet-apple bouquet and lots of generous but crisp fruit in this characterful Champagne. Completely new to me, and a revelation.

ITALY

🍷9 **Concerto Lambrusco Reggiano, Medici Ermete, 2003** **£6.49**

Purple-black colour and lots of fizz to this dry but richly black-fruit exemplar of all that is good about the maligned Lambrusco. Best picnic wine under the sun.

Co-op

Even in the smallest 'market town' Co-op branches belonging to the 2,000-strong chain you will find a decent choice of real quality wines, and in the 'superstores' the selection will run into hundreds of different lines.

A feature of all the own-brand wines is their back labels. It is the Co-op's policy to state all the ingredients in their own wines, and the back labels look very busy on account of it. Co-op Australian Merlot, for example, boasts this ingredient list: 'Grapes, Tartaric acid, Tannin, Preservative (Sulphur Dioxide). Made using: Yeast, Yeast Nutrient (Diammonium phosphate), Copper sulphate, Carbon dioxide, Nitrogen. Cleared using: Filtration, Gelatine, Pectinolytic enzymes.'

Nothing sinister among this lot, I promise, but in an ingredient-conscious world, the Co-op should be congratulated on this kind of openness. No other supermarket – and certainly no other wine retailer, including organic wine specialists – is similarly upfront, and I hope the Co-op is winning lots of new customers on account of it.

ARGENTINA

8 Co-op Argentine Malbec 2004 £3.99
Much improved on previous vintages, this now has relishable fruit as well as characteristic mocha and chocolate darkness.

CHILE

8 Co-op Centalla Pinot Noir 2003 £3.99
Pigeon's eye colour, earthy raspberry aroma and cherry-ripe fruit with balancing dryness and lots of alcohol at 14.5%. Quite a lot of interest for the money.

ITALY

8 Co-op Valpolicella Classico 2003 £4.99
Good dense colour and eager cherry fruit in this well-built lightweight with proper almondy finish.

SOUTH AFRICA

8 Thandi Cabernet-Merlot 2004 £4.99
Strongly blackcurrant nose and pleasingly mellow fruit finishing dry and clean with a bit of gripping tannin. Nice wine made under the Fairtrade scheme.

USA

9 Co-op California Pinot Noir 2004 £4.49
Ripe, pure-fruit strawberry Pinot is immediately appealing. Can't fault the freshness and vigour.

RED WINES   £5 PLUS

AUSTRALIA

🍷8   St Hallet Gamekeeper's Reserve 2004   £5.99
Purply Barossa blend mostly of Shiraz is nicely weighted
with soft but firm grip of the mouth and agreeable spice.
It's 14.5% alcohol and will keep.

FRANCE

🍷8   Blason de Bourgogne Pinot Noir 2003   £6.49
Brisk cherry whiff to this bright, young-tasting Burgundy
brand.

ITALY

🍷8   Caldora Sangiovese 2003   £5.99
Purple brambly Abruzzo red has lush dark fruit with
vanilla notes and good nutskin finish.

NEW ZEALAND

🍷9   Co-op Explorers Vineyard Pinot Noir 2004 £5.99
Enthralling summer soft fruit aroma on this almost-rosé-
pale red, and crisp red fruit flavours. Refreshing and fun.

SOUTH AFRICA

🍷9   Leopards Leap Shiraz 2002   £5.49
Hefty-looking, big-nosed spicy monster (14.5% alcohol)
has long, smooth fruit with underlying baked-earth
character.

PINK WINES	UNDER £5

🍷7 Masterpeace Rosé 2004   £4.49
Bright magenta colour and confectionery nose will give
this wide appeal, and the fruit is drier, livelier and fresher
than the pong suggests.

AUSTRALIA

WHITE WINES	UNDER £5

🍷8 Co-op Island Vines Cyprus White 2004   £3.99
Terribly old-fashioned labelling must hobble sales of this
Co-op perennial, but it's really rather good. It's a dry
wine with a seaside tang to its complex hot-climate fruit.

CYPRUS

🍷8 Co-op Soave Classico 2004   £4.99
Ripe fruit perfume to this flavoursome dry white, and a
good citrus bracer in the fruit. Good example of a wine
that doesn't always do honour to the name.

ITALY

🍷8 Cork Grove Fernão Pires 2004   £4.49
Sappy old-fashioned dry white tailor-made for grilled
fish, preferably sardines.

PORTUGAL

🍷7 Bullion Hill Luscious White 2004   £4.49
'Orange blossom mingles with honey on the nose',
declares the label on this little bit of Californian
sunshine. It's an aromatic off-dry aperitif wine some will
like.

🍷8 Co-op Moses Lake Chardonnay 2004   £4.99
Fruit-blossom nose and richness bordering on the buttery
in this oaked yellow-tasting wine from Washington State.

USA

WHITE WINES	£5 PLUS

AUSTRALIA

🍷10 **St Hallet Poacher's Blend 2004** £5.99
Sunny colour, lush pineapple and mango nose revealing
Sauvignon and Semillon blend (and there's a bit of
Riesling too) followed by scintillating tropical-but-zesty
fruit. Lavishly flavoured and perfumed, yet refreshingly
dry. Fabulous, with modest 11.5% alcohol. Screwcap.

SOUTH AFRICA

🍷8 **Leopards Leap Sauvignon Blanc 2004** £5.49
It's water white, but has a forceful grassy-nettley nose
and crisp green Sauvignon fruit of real zest and length.

SPARKLING WINES	£5 PLUS

FRANCE

🍷9 **Drappier Carte d'Or Brut** £17.99
The Co-op has every right to be proud of this full-
flavoured, brioche-perfumed Champagne. As good as
many much more famous names.

Majestic

This formidable national retailer – or rather wholesaler – goes from strength to strength. Now with 125 branches nationwide, Majestic in the last year has increased its profits by a quarter. This success is deserved, because the range of wines is well chosen and competitively priced. None of the super-markets comes close.

You have to buy at least 12 bottles of wine at a time in Majestic, because it operates under wholesale licences. But this is no hardship, and many of the wines are discounted on the multibuy principle. It might be buy any two or more Italian wines, save 15 per cent on the lot, or buy two of one particular bottle and get 50p, £1 or more off.

Hundreds of wines are promoted in this way at any one time. And all the time, Champagne is discounted by the same means, often dramatically. Recent promotions have included a third off several Champagnes on purchases of three bottles or more.

Not surprising, then, that the average shopper at Majestic spends £113 per visit. You get a lot of good wine for that money. And of the £160 million spent in Majestic over the last year, £7 million was on online sales, via the company's genuinely useful website at **www.majestic.co.uk**.

For those who can't cope with computers, you can simply arm yourself with the all-colour price list and phone an order to the nearest branch, which will happily deliver to your home, at no extra charge.

If I can find fault with Majestic, it's that their branches can be a bit overwhelming. Here must be more than a thousand different wines, not to mention all the beers and spirits, and cases are piled high in canyons that can be too narrow for comfortable navigation behind the jumbo-sized supermarket trolleys provided. There are forests of signs advertising this or that discount, and it can get confusing.

On the other hand, staff are universally well-informed, helpful and enthusiastic – I have been given some very good advice in these stores – and always insist on carrying your purchase to your car.

What supermarket could possibly match that?

CHILE

🍷 9 **Cono Sur Pinot Noir 2004**   **£4.99**
The colour of this perennial classic is extraordinary – it's pale as Pinot Noir reds so often are, but the ruby hue is already taking on a hint of orange, as if this were a much more mature wine. Lovely cherry whiff, a light quaffer (though 13.5% alcohol) with juicy, enduring, refreshing summer-fruit flavour. Real bargain.

🍷 9 **Cuvée de Richard 2004**   **£3.05**
One of the best-value cheapies I've tasted all year. It has a callow colour and the grip of ripe young red from the heat of the far south, but a healthy raspberry aroma and delightfully brambly fruit. Majestic's house red, and very good value indeed.

FRANCE

🍷 8 **Les Marquières Rouge 2004**   **£3.49**
Nice bit of grip and intensity to this briary cheapie. Screwcap.

🍷 9 **Monastier Cabernet Franc 2004**   **£4.99**
Quite dark and dense vin de pays d'Oc has black fruit centre, tannic rim, a hint of pepper and the tell-tale redcurrant twang and leafiness of the Cabernet Franc grape. The Majestic lady tasting alongside me said she liked it too, took another sniff and pronounced 'Chorizo!' See if you agree. Screwcap.

PORTUGAL

🍷 8 **Tagus Creek Syrah/Trincadeira 2004**   **£4.99**
Typical clove-and-cinnamon dark Portuguese everyday red with a panoply of spicy flavours. Try it with grilled fish, especially sardines.

RED WINES   UNDER £5

SPAIN

9 Monte Nisa Merlot 2003   **£2.99**
Seductively sweet entry to this Navarra cheapie morphs into a friendly dry middle fruit with hints of cinnamon and cloves. Light in weight (but 14% alcohol) and fun.

9 Tempranillo La Serrana 2003   **£2.99**
So cheap! It's a decent mouth-filling briar-fruit Barcelona plonk (13.5% alcohol) that really can't be faulted.

RED WINES   £5 PLUS

AUSTRALIA

8 Yering Frog Pinot Noir 2003   **£6.99**
A subtle, even Burgundian, Pinot Noir with sweet, ripe strawberry-raspberry fruit and crisp, firm acidity. From the Yarra Valley, perhaps Australia's best location for Pinot Noir.

9 Sticks Yarra Valley Pinot Noir 2003   **£7.99**
Orangey colour to this grippy and peppery, thoroughly delicious Pinot with an underlying hint of toffee. Very good indeed.

9 Pirramimma Petit Verdot 2001   **£9.49**
'Abundant violet spicy aromas' declares the back label note on this dark and hugely fruity McLaren Vale giant in the super-ripe Bordeaux mode (with 14.5% alcohol). Brilliantly balanced, exciting food wine.

8 Willunga Creek Black Duck
Cabernet Sauvignon Merlot 2003   **£9.99**
Bible black colour to this soupy, liquorice monster with a nicely contrived finish and 14% alcohol. For the serious barbecue.

CHILE

8 Casillero del Diablo Shiraz 2004   £5.49
Richly concentrated black fruit style put me in mind of
the kind of syrup poured over ice cream, except that this
is not overripe (though 14% alcohol) and finishes clean
and dry.

FRANCE

9 Mas Las Cabes, Jean Gardiès, 2003   £6.49
Dense, rich colour to this gutsy, peppery Roussillon red is
matched by its intensity of dark, gripping fruit.

8 Domaine de la Janasse
Terre de Bussière 2003   £7.49
Robust spicy Rhône from notoriously hot 2003 vintage is
just the OK side of jammy, with 14.5% alcohol and
buckets of black fruit. Good winter warmer.

8 Pinot Noir Valmoissine, Louis Latour, 2002 £7.49
Light colour is already browning in this earthy, sweet-
cherry southern Pinot with rather elegant and restrained
soft summer fruitiness.

10 Saumur-Champigny Les Tuffeaux,
Château de Targé, 2003   £7.55
Fruit bomb from the Loire has real Cabernet Franc
character, with ripeness and a crunchy edge to the fruit.
Good food wine, to match tricky items like asparagus or
salads. Truly distinctive red of great quality and
character.

8 Bourgogne Rouge Vieilles Vignes,
Domaine Sarrazin, 2003   £7.99
Pale, with pleasing strawberry nose and eager, bright red
fruit flavours to this approachable 'ordinary' burgundy.

FRANCE

8   **Perrin Rasteau L'Andéol 2003**   £8.99
Top-quality Rhône village red has plenty of grunt (14% alcohol) and a touch of velvet.

8   **Bourgogne Côte Chalonnaise Les Gorgères, Michel Sarrazin, 2002**   £9.99
Healthy crimson colour, seductive cherry smell and well-formed gripping earthy summer fruit. Could well develop for a year or two.

9   **St Paul de Dominique 2001**   £11.99
This St Emilion Grand Cru seems unusually 'forward' for its age. But I can't fault its handsome bricky colour, lush, cool and intense cedar-cassis fruit and sheer elegance.

10   **Givry 1er Cru Vieilles Vignes, Domaine Sarrazin, 2003**   £12.99
Lovely strawberry whiff and buckets of plump soft fruit with extravagant vanilla richness in this superb, ready-to-drink burgundy from the often-marvellous Givry AC. Amazing luxuriance of Pinot Noir fruit, and a great treat. You'll come immediately under the burgundy spell.

8   **La Réserve de Léoville Barton 2000**   £19.99
From one of Bordeaux's top estates and a greatly esteemed vintage, this still has a bitter-chocolate centre to its sumptuous fruit, and will develop for years. Definitely going places.

ITALY

8   **Dogajolo Carpineto 2003**   £7.99
Dark, baked fruit in this dense Tuscan red has a good cutting edge of acidity.

RED WINES   £5 PLUS

ITALY

🍷8 **Barolo Pio Cesare 2000**   £29.00
Show-off's wine is the colour of oloroso sherry, has the spirity nose typical of Barolo, and that curious mix of delicate red fruit and tannic grip. Might improve with age.

NEW ZEALAND

🍷8 **Farleigh Estate Pinot Noir 2003**   £9.99
Keen sweet summer-fruit nose and dense, spicy, satisfying fruit very much in the Kiwi style. It's 14.5% alcohol and has a screwcap.

SOUTH AFRICA

🍷9 **Fairview Peg Leg Carignan 2003**   £7.99
Lovely creamy bright-fruit soft red with good balance and 14% alcohol.

🍷10 **Vergelegen Cabernet Sauvignon 2001**   £13.99
Blackcurrants bursting with ripeness under the sun are encapsulated in the aroma and flavour of this epic Cape red. It is simply wonderful, an unnerving 15% alcohol, but by no means daunting. Mature, perfectly poised and one of the best wines from anywhere I've tasted in years.

SPAIN

🍷8 **Durius Tempranillo, Arribes del Duero,**
      2003   £6.99
Lush, dark flavours with vanilla oakiness and spiky highlights in this popular branded red. Very satisfying indeed.

PINK WINES	UNDER £5

ARGENTINA

🍷9 **Finca Las Moras Shiraz Rosé 2004** £4.99
Bold magenta, blackberry fruit, clean crunchy style. Tops for value. Screwcap.

FRANCE

🍷7 **Pinot Grigio Rosé 'Adagio' 2004** £4.69
Pink PG! How can it fail? It's a mystery how they make rosé wine from white grapes, but this has a nice pale onion skin colour, soft, boiled-sweet nose and crowd-pleasing matching flavour.

PINK WINES	£5 PLUS

CHILE

🍷8 **Santa Rita Cabernet Sauvignon
Rosé 2004** £5.85
Luminous colour, brisk, crunchy blackcurrant style.

🍷8 **Rosé de Flaugergues 2004** £6.45
Cheery shocking pink Languedoc confection with crispness and freshness. Screwcap.

FRANCE

🍷8 **Château de Sours Rosé 2004** £8.99
Posh Bordeaux pink has magenta colour, gripping strawberry fruit and enough interest for the money. Screwcap, amazingly enough.

WHITE WINES   UNDER £5

ARGENTINA

7 **Argento Pinot Grigio 2004**   £4.99
Every wine nation is leaping aboard the PG bandwagon and this attempt is as good as anything from Italy at the price. Plenty of ripe fruit and 13.5% alcohol.

CHILE

8 **Casillero del Diablo Chardonnay 2004**   £4.99
Pineapple whiff and fruit-salad dimension to this rather rich and contemplative wine with 13.5% alcohol.

9 **Cuvée de Richard Blanc 2004**   £3.05
Majestic's house white from the Toulouse vin de pays zone has a floral nose, good tangy fruit and plenty of interest. Bargain.

8 **Les Marquières Blanc 2004**   £3.49
Plenty of crisp top flavour in this dry deep-south refresher.

FRANCE

8 **Domaine Vieux Manoir de Maransan 2004** £4.99
Dry but assertive sunny Rhône white has an undercurrent of exotic richness.

8 **Saumur Blanc Réserve des Vignerons 2004** £4.99
Well-ripened flinty dry white has good sunny intensity – unusually interesting for this dull Loire appellation.

ITALY

9 **Gavi Terredavino 2004**   £4.99
Nice note of nectar on the nose of this exotic dry Piedmont white, followed up by layered fruit-salad flavours.

WHITE WINES	£5 PLUS

CHILE

8 **Late Harvest Sauvignon Blanc,
Concha y Toro, 2001 half bottle** £4.69
Clever marriage of honey fruit and lemon edge in this easy-drinking stickie, to sip with blue cheese if not with puds.

9 **Cono Sur Gewürztraminer 2004** £5.49
Well-contrived exotic but by no means oversweet lychee-perfumed aperitif wine in the Alsace style, with 13.5% alcohol.

8 **Montes Reserve Sauvignon Blanc 2004** £5.59
Agricultural, assertive style to this asparagussy Sauvignon.

FRANCE

7 **Grand Ardèche Chardonnay,
Louis Latour, 2002** £7.49
Southern vin de pays under name of grand Burgundy maker Louis Latour has old-fashioned 'buttery' style that will appeal to some drinkers more than it does to me.

9 **Quincy Jean-Charles Borgnat 2004** £7.49
Asparagus dominates the nose on this fine Loire Sauvignon, with a cheery bit of dungheap alongside. Super green-fruit refresher with complexity and length of flavour from an appellation commonly called 'poor man's Sancerre'.

8 **Pouilly-Fumé Les Rabichottes,
Fournier, 2004** £8.49
Very intense Loire Sauvignon with crisp but lingering gooseberry-nettle flavour.

9 **Sancerre Domaine Gérard Fiou 2004** £8.99
Nettley but rather rich Sauvignon style is a bargain for this fashionable Loire appellation.

WHITE WINES	£5 PLUS

FRANCE

 **Mâcon-Fuissé Vieilles Vignes,
Christophe Cordier, 2004** £10.99
Well constructed sumptuous southern Burgundy with complexity and length.

ITALY

 Roero Arneis 2004 £5.99
Brisk peary fruit with good malic acidity in this interesting dry wine.

 **Riff Pinot Grigio delle Venezie,
Alois Legeder, 2004** £6.99
Generous fruit in this smoky-tangy, mouthfilling PG. Worth trading up for.

NEW ZEALAND

 Farleigh Estate Sauvignon Blanc 2004 £6.99
Relatively speaking, a softer style, with retreating acidity, for a Kiwi Sauvignon. Will appeal to those who don't like their dry whites too 'sharp'. Screwcap.

Southbank Estate Sauvignon Blanc 2004 £6.99
Brisk, nettle-fresh, fruit-packed style with limey acidity. Very good value. Screwcap.

Farleigh Estate Riesling 2004 £7.99
If you haven't tried Kiwi Riesling, start here. Seductive, limey but lushly ripe food wine (grilled prawns, fish pie, roast chicken) of real character.

WHITE WINES	£5 PLUS

PORTUGAL

8 **Quinta de Azevedo Vinho Verde 2004** £5.49
Prickly-crisp dry 'green wine', once very popular, is a welcome rarity.

SOUTH AFRICA

9 **Vergelegen Chardonnay 2003** £7.99
Vergelegen is one of the Stellenbosch region's top wineries, and this 'everyday' shardy lives up to the name – big caramel nose, but quite restrained, crisp apple fruit of real class.

SPAIN

8 **Albariño Rias Baixas, Martin Codax, 2004** £8.49
Chi-chi dry white in the Sauvignon Blanc style is glitteringly refreshing.

FRANCE

 9   **Piper Heidsieck Demi Sec NV**   **£20.99**

You can tell only from the taste, and not the smell, that this is a 'dessert' Champagne. Many drinkers will probably just think it's a bit less acidic than others, and few would call it sweet. I loved its gentle softness and honey hint, finding it no less stimulating than the brisk, bone-dry brut style. Good food matcher, and good value on Majestic deals such as the one at the time of writing: buy three, pay £13.99 each.

8   **Nicolas Feuillatte Cuvée Spéciale**
      Brut 1998   **£25.49**

Immediately appealing vintage Champagne with maturity and mouthfilling flavours of buttered toast with apple freshness is a bargain on deals such as the one at the time of writing: buy three, pay £16.99.

8   **Laurent Perrier Ultra Brut**   **£31.99**

Ultra Brut means this Champagne has had very little sweetening at the last stage of the process in which a 'dosage' of sugar and wine is added to top up the bottle after the 'disgorging' of the lees (the yeasty remnants of the in-bottle fermentation that gives the wine its fizz). The style is certainly dry but not green, and the fruit is deliciously crisp. It's a bit lower in calories than usual brut, if you really care. At the time of writing, the deal on this was buy two, pay £23.99.

🍷10 **Perrier-Jouët Brut 1998**
£35.99

Tastes are very personal when it comes to Champagne, but this is the one I have liked best all year. It has the enticing 'biscuity' aroma of mature Champagne that has spent a long time on its lees and a sinfully rich, vivacious style. This is true quality, true luxury. Don't buy this Champagne one bottle at a time. Majestic invariably offer huge discounts for modest 'bulk'. At the time of writing, this PJ was being offered at a third off, £23.99 each, if you bought three bottles or more. That's the same price as some non-vintage Champagnes that are not even half as good.

FRANCE

🍷7 **Pinot Grigio Brut Sachetto**
£7.49

Rather sweet, and barely recognisable as PG, but a vigorously sparkling and jolly fizz that's an improvement on Asti. If the third-off deal for three bottles, reducing the price to £4.99, continues, it's a good buy.

ITALY

—Marks & Spencer—

Marks & Spencer's wines are decidedly different from the crowd. While other grocery giants' shelves are filled largely with global brands – and progressively more so, it seems – every wine here is an 'own-label' product unique to M&S.

I am not entirely sure whether this is an advantage for Marks or not. On the plus side, the M&S name is no doubt a strong suggestion, if not a guarantee, of quality. But it's surely a minus that the stores have none of the heavily advertised bestselling brands such as Blossom Hill and Gallo from California or Hardys and Penfolds of Australia on their shelves.

But this is the way they do things at Marks, and there's no sign, in spite of the chain's much-reported troubles, of any sort of change. And as far as the quality of the wines goes, I can report that it's all looking pretty good. The lack of famous names in no way diminishes the choice or the interest. Quite the opposite, in fact.

RED WINES   UNDER £5

ARGENTINA

8 **El Dueño Shiraz 2004**   £4.99
Hint of hot bitumen in this tannic purple-bright red but sleek, minty fruit too. Good purposeful food wine.

CHILE

8 **Casablanca Valley Pinot Noir 2004**   £4.99
Typical earthy Chilean Pinot has a nice streak of strawberry.

FRANCE

9 **Gold Label Cabernet Sauvignon 2004**   £4.99
Perennial M&S bargain from the Languedoc has plump but well-defined blackcurranty style with crisp rim of acidity. Excellent 'everyday' wine.

9 **Grenache Noir Vin de Pays des Côtes Catalanes 2004**   £4.99
Super southern glugger with spice and grip (and 14.5% alcohol) has upfront fruit rather in the Aussie manner, but without jamminess.

SOUTH AFRICA

8 **Dolphin Bay Shiraz 2004**   £3.99
Lurid colour, gripping and leathery flavour, but very drinkable in a macho sort of way.

8 **Trackers Trail Shiraz 2004**   £4.99
Chewy monster (14.5% alcohol) has big bright red-fruit first flavour and quite modest weight.

SPAIN

8 **La Basca Uvas Tintos 2004**   £4.99
Lurid mauve colour, cheery confectionery nose and plenty of ripe, blackcurrant fruit.

RED WINES — £5 PLUS

9 Dorrien Estate Shiraz 2003 £7.99
Dark-hearted coaly monster with 15% alcohol is spicy
and plush, hefty yet poised. Very, very likeable. Good
with roast lamb.

9 Lenbridge Forge Pinot Noir 2004 £7.99
From the Yarra Valley in Victoria, but you'd more likely
guess it's European, even Burgundian. Pale but
interesting colour, warm strawberry-raspberry whiff, nice
pure, slightly earthy fruit. Lush yet delicate; try it with
fish pie or roast pork.

9 Shady Grove Cabernet Sauvignon 2001 £13.99
Luxury intense black-fruit wine has an artful balance of
restraint and effusion, and 14.5% alcohol. Super stuff for
a special dinner, ideally of beef.

8 Casa Leona Reserve Cabernet Sauvignon
2003 £6.50
Big black-fruit gripper has a friendly tannic finish, 14%
alcohol and satisfying weight.

8 Secano Estate Pinot Noir 2004 £6.99
Plush, silky-minty oaked smoothie has 14% alcohol and
intense cherry fruit.

8 Leon de Oro Merlot Cabernet Sauvignon
2003 £9.99
Rich creamy cassis nose on this dense, purple-black
young-tasting wine leads on to a hugely enjoyable minty-
cedary blackcurrant fruit. Luxury wine and 14.5%
alcohol.

AUSTRALIA

CHILE

FRANCE

🍷 8   **Corbières Gérard Bertrand 2003**   £5.49
Rather a sweetie from a Languedoc appellation that can be a bit tough and overripe, especially in broiling vintages like 2003.

🍷 9   **Minervois Gerard Bertrand 2003**   £5.49
Dark and dense red from a very hot vintage in the Languedoc is nevertheless obligingly fruity and definitely not 'cooked'. Excellent wine from an appellation that cannot always be counted on.

🍷 10   **Côtes de Nuits Villages 2002**   £9.99
Shamelessly seductive burgundy from the environs of the great wine town of Nuits St Georges. As an introduction to the inimitable summer-fruit style and poised elegance of burgundy, this is perfect.

🍷 8   **Domaine Bunan Bandol 2001**   £11
Fashionable red of the Côte d'Azur is plummy and dark and still needs three or four years to balance the generous fruit and encroaching tannin.

🍷 9   **Initial de Desmirail Margaux 2002**   £12.99
Château Desmirail is a *grand cru classé* estate of Bordeaux and this is its 'second' wine made from parts of the harvest not required for the *grand vin* itself. But it certainly tastes like classic claret, deliciously ripe and balanced, and already drinking well.

🍷 9   **Pommard 2003**   £20
Grand burgundy from a famed village is by no means overpriced. Cerebral strawberry-scented soft-fruit Pinot Noir of lovely silkiness and intensity.

RED WINES   £5 PLUS

10 **Chianti Burchino 2003**   £6.99

I love Chianti, but it's too often anonymous, or overpriced. This one is neither. It has inky darkness, a proper bristling, nutty, brambly nose and lashings of vigorous, dark, concentrated plummy fruit. Real Chianti, and great value.

ITALY

8 **Chianti Colli Fiorentini 2003**   £7.99

If you can't find the prodigious Chianti above (it's not in every store) look for this one, from the hills of Florence. It's dark, edgy and stimulating, ideal with pasta.

8 **Kaituna Hills Merlot Cabernet 2003**   £6.99

This has the hallmark eucalyptus mintiness in the fruit of red Kiwi wines, with silkiness and pure-fruit ripeness. Distinctive.

NEW ZEALAND

8 **Vinha Padro Pedro 2003**   £5.99

Leafy, stalky whiffs from this Ribatejo wine lead on to a remarkably defined minty dark fruit of classic Portuguese character.

8 **Quinta de Fafide 2003**   £7.99

Table wine from port country, the Douro Valley, is deep purple with concentrated blackcurrant flavours very close to port. Lovely meaty stuff.

PORTUGAL

RED WINES   £5 PLUS

SOUTH AFRICA

🍷9 Houdamond Pinotage 2004   £7.99
There's a kind of lanolin richness to this brambly blockbuster (13.5% alcohol) with vanilla oakiness and black-fruit sweetness, and the distinctive style of the Cape's own Pinotage grape. Distinctive and delicious.

SPAIN

🍷8 Las Almenas 2002   £5.49
Cool, pure-fruit edgy tannic red with clean berry fruit. Interesting and good.

🍷8 Pago Real Rioja 2002   £11
Dusky, gently browning colour to this vanilla-smooth, cassis-fruit intense red, with dark chocolate centre. Softly tannic and deliciously gripping.

PINK WINES   UNDER £5

SPAIN

🍷8 Las Falleras Rosé 2004   £3.29
Very cheap, but convincingly fruity and refreshing.

🍷7 Torresoto Rioja Rosé 2004   £4.99
Crisp, uncomplicated pink from Garnacha grapes has summer fruit and freshness.

Pink Wines — £5 plus

FRANCE

8 Domaine de Verlaque Rosé 2004 — £5.99
From Provence, an appropriately sunny, bright pink with rose petals in the smell and generous concentration of strawberry fruit in the flavour.

8 Rosé d'Anjou NV — £5.99
Very pale magenta and just 10.5% alcohol, this non-vintage Loire Valley pink nevertheless delivers a considerable punch of straight strawberry fruit.

ITALY

8 La Prendina Estate Rosé 2004 — £5.99
Nice coral colour to this, but you only see it when you pour out a glassful, because M&S bottle their rosés in green glass. I thought the colour of these wines was a large part of their shelf appeal, but Marks obviously don't think so. This one has a crisp, soft-fruit style and tastes as good as it looks.

White Wines — Under £5

ARGENTINA

8 El Dueño Chardonnay 2004 — £4.99
Rich, rather old-fashioned coconutty oaked Chardonnay is fun.

FRANCE

7 Vin de Pays d'Oc Sauvignon Blanc 2004 — £4.99
Economy Sauvignon from the south is crisp and well-defined, and comes in a grand, heavy bottle.

WHITE WINES   UNDER £5

GERMANY

♈9   **Pinot Grigio 2004**   **£4.99**
They've shoehorned a lot of fruit salad and zest into this big-flavoured (and 13.5% alcohol) Rhine refresher, which is among the best PGs I've found at under a fiver this year.

ITALY

♈8   **Aramonte Catarratto 2004**   **£4.99**
Unusually interesting lush but dry and grassy wine from Sicily's pedestrian Catarratto grape – effect is like Muscadet, but with flavour.

♈8   **Verdicchio dei Castelli di Jesi 2004**   **£4.99**
This does have some distinctiveness, with a blossomy perfume and green, herbaceous fruit.

♈7   **Via Ulivi Pinot Grigio 2004**   **£4.99**
Lemony, light PG from the Veneto region has freshness.

SOUTH AFRICA

♈8   **Dolphin Bay Sauvignon Blanc 2005**   **£3.99**
Tangy lemon first flavour is followed by a good whack of gooseberry fruit and refreshing zest. Bargain.

♈8   **Trackers Trail Sauvignon Blanc 2004**   **£4.99**
Distinct asparagus nose and more of the same in the crisp, nettley fruit. Fresh and relishable.

WHITE WINES	£5 PLUS

AUSTRALIA

8 **Langhorne Creek Estate Pinot Grigio 2004** **£7.99**
This comes in a silly amphora-shaped, flange-topped bottle, but it's nevertheless an outstanding PG. Briskly fresh, smoky-spicy dry white craftily spiked with a bit of Sauvignon Blanc.

CHILE

8 **Secano Estate Sauvignon Blanc 2004** **£6.99**
Tangy, bright, crisp gooseberry style is arrestingly good. Well above the standard for Chilean Sauvignon.

FRANCE

7 **Alsace Gewürztraminer 2004** **£6.99**
Lychee-scented, exotically spicy and lush but not too sweet, from ubiquitous Turckheim co-operative that seems to supply just about all the UK supermarkets.

8 **Meursault 2003** **£20**
The real thing, and authentically expensive, this is a lavish oaked Chardonnay with proper Burgundian complexity and restraint. A nifty introduction to the style.

GERMANY

8 **Darting Estate Michelsberg Riesling 2004** **£5.99**
Bumper fresh hock with density and length. Screwcap.

9 **Mineralstein Riesling 2004** **£5.99**
Crisp and lively aperitif moselle has plenty of the 'mineral' character suggested by the name. Screwcap.

10 **Ernst Loosen Erdener Treppchen**
Riesling Kabinett 2004 **£9.99**
Quite a honeyed style to the rushing, racy classic Riesling fruit in this fabulously balanced moselle. Note just 7.5% alcohol. Screwcap.

WHITE WINES   £5 PLUS

ITALY

9 **Friuli Sauvignon 2004**   £5.99
What a delicious surprise this is. Italian Sauvignon is a
scarce commodity, yet here is one with real *brio* – lively,
crisp, grassy dry white of a standard to compare even
with Kiwi counterparts.

8 **La Prendina Estate Pinot Grigio 2004**   £6.99
More evidence that if you pay the right money, you can
get decent PG. This one from Lake Garda is in the
aromatic style with green fruit and a hint of smoke.

NEW ZEALAND

9 **Kaituna Hills Chardonnay 2004**   £5.99
Consistently good M&S brand has likeable cabbagey
whiff and straight, lush Chardonnay fruit. Very well
made.

10 **Kaituna Hills Reserve Sauvignon Blanc
2004**   £7.99
Truly vivid wine with asparagus and nettles on the nose,
matching flavours and limey finish. An exceptional wine
even by Kiwi standards, and keenly priced.

9 **Clocktower Sauvignon Blanc 2004**   £9.99
Lovely wine, which I can most adequately describe as an
enriched version of the Kaituna Hills Sauvignon
described above.

SPARKLING WINES   £5 PLUS

8 **Oudinot Champagne Brut**   **£16.99**

Marks's own-brand champers seems to have much more brioche dimension and fullness of fruit than I remember from before. Greatly improved.

8 **Duc D'Ambleny Champagne 1999**   **£25**

Lots of ripeness in this vintage Champagne, which I discover has been aged, in its still-wine stage, in Sauternes barrels. Rich but dry, and quite distinctive. For those who don't like their champers too green or 'sharp'.

8 **Asti Spumante**   **£5.99**

Very muscatty (like table grapes) but manageably balanced between sweetness and freshness, with good persistent fizz and just 7.5% alcohol.

7 **Pinot Grigio Brut**   **£6.99**

White Pinot Grigio wines are enduringly popular, and sparkling wine sales continue to soar, and so to sparkling Pinot Grigio. Perhaps this will sell well. It's quite soft, properly fizzy, and even tastes vaguely like PG.

9 **Prosecco**   **£6.99**

Very fashionable softly fizzy dry white has pear juice smell, good mousse, and a really delightful orchard-fruit style. Balanced and very refreshing, it took me completely by surprise.

Morrisons

Even before Morrisons performed the remarkable trick of swallowing another supermarket chain twice its own size in 2004, this Yorkshire-based company was boasting that its wine sales have been increasing by a fifth every year. That's about eight times faster than your average supermarket chain – including the newly subsumed Safeway, no doubt.

How do they do it? Well, Morrisons have some unique selling points when it comes to wine. One is that they offer 100 different wines costing under £3. Another is that they only sell wines that sell. Or, to put it another way, they don't bother with wines that have only a minority appeal. This largely explains why so many of the Safeway wines I hoped they would retain have in fact disappeared. Maybe I was the only customer buying them.

The upshot is that the choice of wine in the newly combined Morrison-Safeway range is a limited one. With 560 lines, it sounds numerically diverse, but this is the same size the Morrisons range was before the takeover. The 850 wines Safeway brought to the party have been reduced to very few indeed.

Nevertheless, Morrisons is a keenly competitive wine retailer, and among the inevitable ranks of global brands, there are plenty of interesting wines, some of them remarkably cheap, that are well worth seeking out.

RED WINES   UNDER £5

FRANCE

🍷 **8**   Château Le Pin 2003   £4.99
There is another Château Le Pin in Bordeaux, which makes the world's most expensive wine. This one is therefore good for a giggle, and delicious, too – dark, vigorous, sappy, and 14% alcohol.

ITALY

🍷 **8**   Soltero Sicilia Rosso NV   £2.99
Bargain warmly fruity soft but healthy glugging red from Sicily's giant Settesoli co-op is perhaps not typical of the island's usual roast-fruit style, but very pleasant.

🍷 **9**   Fior di Vigna Montepulciano d'Abruzzo, Uggiano, 2003   £4.29
Deliciously vigorous briary bright slurper has true balance of dark fruit with eager acidity. Drink cool as an outdoor aperitif, or as it comes with sticky pasta dishes – which it will 'cut' perfectly.

WHITE WINES   UNDER £5

FRANCE

🍷 **9**   Preiss-Zimmer Pinot Blanc 2003   £4.99
Lush limpid herbaceous-vegetal Alsace dry white of great character is a bargain.

WHITE WINES	£5 PLUS

AUSTRALIA

9 Brown Brothers Late Harvested Muscat 2004 £5.99

Golden wine rich with opulent grapy ripeness, and yet light in weight, just 11% alcohol and finishing with fresh, pure crispness.

9 Jacob's Creek Reserve Chardonnay 2003 £7.99

There's no getting away from it. This is a big brand name, perhaps the biggest, but it is fabulous wine, a masterly marriage of luxury fruit with mineral, citrus acidity. Tastes like a very expensive wine indeed.

FRANCE

8 Preiss-Zimmer Gewürztraminer 2004 £5.99

Aromatic and extravagantly exotic Alsace medium-dry white is well balanced by its acidity. Popular choice with oriental food, but an inspired aperitif wine too. Screwcap.

J Sainsbury

The supermarket that invented own-label wines back in the 1970s still has the best range of these, and this is reflected among the descriptions that follow. The first wine mentioned, an own-label from Argentina, is the bargain of the year, and there are 20 more excellent buys from both the old world and new. The quality of these wines is encouraging, because they are an antidote to the boring global brands that take up so much space on the shelves, and reassuring evidence that Sainsbury's wine team are out there sourcing good stuff they like and trust sufficiently to stick their own name on it.

RED WINES UNDER £5

ARGENTINA

🍷**10** Sainsbury's Argentinian Bonarda NV   £3.49
Soft and seductive plump ripe blackberry red is simply delicious and cannot be bettered at this price.

AUSTRALIA

🍷**7** Sainsbury's Australian Ruby
Cabernet Shiraz 2004   £2.80
Improbable price, but worth trying for its firmly friendly blackberry fruit, with 14% alcohol.

🍷**8** Sainsbury's Bin 60 Australia
Cabernet Shiraz 2004   £4.99
Opaque darkness of colour and 14.5% alcohol make for densely concentrated dark-fruit flavours with pepper seasoning.

CHILE

🍷**9** Sainsbury's Reserve Selection Chilean
Cabernet Sauvignon 2004   £4.99
Super intensity of cassis fruit in this blockbuster (14% alcohol) mature-tasting food red with briary vigour. Good balance.

🍷**8** Sainsbury's Reserve Selection Chilean
Carmenère 2003   £4.99
Bracing blackcurrant fruit with dark heart to the flavour has lingering aftertaste. You warm to it.

FRANCE

🍷**9** La Chasse du Pape Syrah 2004   £4.99
I'm a fan of this ubiquitous Languedoc brand. It's deep purple, generously ripe and spicy and great value.

🍷**8** Reserve des Tuileries 2004   £4.99
Dark, briary Roussillon seasoned with pepper, to match saucissons and starchy foods.

Red Wines — Under £5

SPAIN

9 **Gran Garnacha 2004** £2.99
Clean-tasting bramble-fruit glugger from Cariñena is thoroughly Spanish and relishable, and very cheap.

8 **Los Monteros 2003** £4.99
Plump ripe red-berry fruit in this sunny Valencian red.

Red Wines — £5 Plus

ARGENTINA

8 **Weinert Malbec 1999** £7.49
Spicy black-fruit tarry gripper still has tannic edge in spite of great age (by New World standards) and might well round out to something extraordinary with another couple of years in bottle. I've written down 'hamburger wine' but mean no harm by it.

AUSTRALIA

9 **Sainsbury's Classic Selection**
Western Australian Cabernet Merlot 2003 £6.99
Pitch black, rich cassis nose and ripe, sleek, minty dark fruit. Dare I say it has the elegance of a decent Bordeaux as well as the whoomph of Aussie upfront fruit?

CHILE

8 **Don Reca Merlot Limited Release 2002** £8.99
Frightfully smart bottle with correspondingly grand wine of luxury ripeness lives up to its own description of 'mocha coffee, dark chocolate, pepper and sweet plum flavours'. Note 14.5% alcohol.

8 **Casa Lapostolle Cuvée Alexandre**
Merlot 2002 £12.99
Chile doesn't do much wine at this elevated level, but this one is a good flag-flyer. Colour is still a bit raw, but the nose and fruit are coming on nicely, showing intense concentration and ripeness (14.5% alcohol) but elegant restraint. Keep it a couple more years for a real treat.

RED WINES £5 PLUS

FRANCE

**🍷8 Sainsbury's Classic Selection
Beaujolais Villages 2004** £5.99
Purple bright wine with a really bouncy jammy-Gamay fruit. It actually tastes like Beaujolais (which lots don't).

**🍷8 Sainsbury's Classic Selection
Vintage Claret 2004** £5.99
Not as lean as it looks, this is a firmly fruity and softly tannic quality Bordeaux for drinking, and enjoying, now.

**🍷8 Capitel dei Nicalo Valpolicella Classico
Superiore Appassimento Breve 2003** £6.99
Sweet cherry perfume and plump, dense sunny fruit in this rather grand example, rounded off with a fine dry almonds-with-skins-on finish.

🍷9 Brolio Chianti Classico 2002 £10.99
Dark, bitter-chocolate centre to the flavour of this gripping cherry-mocha heavyweight (13.5% alcohol) from the estate where the Chianti formula was first devised 150 years ago.

ITALY

**🍷8 Sainsbury's Classic Selection
Amarone della Valpolicella 2002** £10.99
Pitch-black edgy monster (14.5% alcohol) has plummy-raspberry topnotes and vanilla and spice below in the infinite, dry-finishing depths. Great cheese matcher.

🍷8 Sainsbury's Classic Selection Barolo 2000 £10.99
Supermarkets insist on selling Italy's most prestigious red, but most of it is rubbish. This one, from big producer Ascheri, isn't bad. Colour as wan as usual and going orange with age, and good roasty, near-spirity fruit with authentic rose-petal aroma and 13.5% alcohol.

RED WINES   £5 PLUS

NEW ZEALAND

9 **Delegat's Oyster Bay Merlot 2004**   £7.99
Slinky, minty 'cool-climate' Merlot made the way only
the Kiwis know how. If you haven't discovered this new
class of Merlot, get acquainted via this one.

9 **Sherwood Estate Pinot Noir 2003**   £7.99
Very emphatic strawberry style to this elegant Pinot with
ethereal weight and lush silkiness. Good price, but only
from Sainsbury online.

SOUTH AFRICA

8 **The Wolftrap 2004**   £5.99
Baked fruit with a hint of hot tyres makes for an
intriguingly savoury and muscular (14.5% alcohol) red.

9 **Boschendal Shiraz 2002**   £6.99
Big brand delivers the goods. It's clean and brisk as well
as meatily intense (14% alcohol) and spicy and really
does the job.

8 **Muruve Roble Toro 2003**   £5.99
Black, even tarry, middle fruit in this robust ripe red with
14% alcohol.

SPAIN

8 **Carmesi Oak Aged Garnacha Tempranillo**
2003   £6.99
Ingratiating smoothie from Calatayud region (renowned
for stonking reds) is intensely satisfying, 14.5% alcohol,
and just the thing with roast pork.

8 **Durius Tempranillo, Arribes del Duero**
2003   £6.99
Lush, dark flavours with vanilla oakiness and spiky
highlights in this popular branded red. Very satisfying
indeed.

RED WINES   £5 PLUS

SPAIN

10 **Sainsbury's Classic Selection Rioja**
Reserva Elegia 1999   £8.49
Good price for Rioja as lofty as this. It's thoroughly
mature, going orange at the rim and with vanilla notes
and orange peel on the nose. Lovely weight of fruit with
proper gentility of Rioja. Lovely example of one of the
world's classic wine styles.

USA

8 **Ravenswood Lodi Old Vine Zinfandel**
2002   £7.99
Well-structured rather Cabernet-like luxury red from
California's protean indigenous grape, with 14.5%
alcohol.

PINK WINES   UNDER £5

FRANCE

9 **Cabernet Rosé VdP Jardin de la France**
2004   £3.89
Pale coral colour, fresh but sweetly summer-fruit
flavoured and altogether charming. Likeable, affordable,
Loire Valley pink.

SOUTH AFRICA

7 **Cape Grace Pinotage Rosé 2005**   £4.49
Magenta confectionery-nosed ripe pink with 13.5%
alcohol from South Africa's indigenous black grape
variety.

SPAIN

8 **Agramont Garnacha Rosado 2004**   £3.99
Crisp magenta with brisk strawberry fruit from Navarra.

PINK WINES   £5 PLUS

FRANCE

🍷8 **Domaine de Sours Rosé 2004**   **£5.49**
Deep pink colour, good concentration of soft summer fruit, crisp finish.

WHITE WINES   UNDER £5

ARGENTINA

🍷8 **Sainsbury's Argentinian Torrontes NV**   **£3.49**
Good density of Muscat-table-grape type fruit in this ethnic cheapie.

AUSTRALIA

🍷8 **Sainsbury's Australian Colombard Chardonnay 2004**   **£2.99**
Perfectly clean, fresh dry wine with decent lift of acidity. Price can only be wondered at.

🍷8 **Sainsbury's Bin 20 Australian Chardonnay 2004**   **£4.99**
Soft, appley style with well-corrected finish.

CHILE

🍷9 **Cono Sur Gewürztraminer 2003**   **£4.99**
Exotic lychee nose, fruit-salad flavours and a neat balance between residual sweetness and citrus acidity.

FRANCE

🍷8 **Prestige du Roc Sauvignon Blanc 2004**   **£4.49**
Bargain-price Bordeaux straight-fruit grassy dry white.

🍷9 **Première Touraine Sauvignon Blanc 2004**   **£4.79**
Gooseberries and grassy freshness are evoked in this well-made Loire wine with liveliness and dimension.

WHITE WINES   UNDER £5

FRANCE

🍷8 **Sainsbury's Classic Selection Muscadet
Sèvre et Maine sur Lie 2000**   £4.99
Nice floral bloom in the nose of this creditable tangy, sea-breeze fresh and manageably citric bone-dry Loire white. Ideal with, and in, moules marinière.

NEW ZEALAND

🍷9 **Sainsbury's New Zealand Sauvignon Blanc
2004**   £4.99
The first Kiwi Sauvignon I've found under a fiver, and it's pretty good – green fruit, real rush of tangy, grassy flavour and unmistakably in the glittering NZ style.

WHITE WINES   £5 PLUS

AUSTRALIA

🍷8 **Sainsbury's Classic Selection Padthaway
Chardonnay 2004**   £6.99
Big, concentrated vegetal wine with deluxe appeal by good McLaren Vale producer Tatachilla. Insinuatingly delicious.

🍷9 **Jacob's Creek Reserve Chardonnay 2003**   £7.99
There's no getting away from it. This is a big brand name, perhaps the biggest, but it is fabulous wine, a masterly marriage of luxury fruit with mineral, citrus acidity. Tastes like a very expensive wine indeed.

CHILE

🍷8 **El Dorado Sauvignon Blanc Reserva 2004**   £6.99
This is like a ritzy version of the elegant and restrained Bordeaux Sauvignon style rather than an attempt to ape the world-conquering New Zealand approach.

WHITE WINES	£5 PLUS

CHILE

**8 Casa Lapostolle Cuvée Alexandre
Chardonnay 2003**   £9.99
Yellow wine with pineapple, banana and more on the
nose, plus correspondingly lavish, creamy flavours and
14.5% alcohol. But not just for footballers' wives – it has
cerebral appeal too.

FRANCE

8 Sainsbury's Classic Selection Vouvray 2004 £5.99
Mango-ripe, lush but dry finishing Chenin Blanc from a
great Loire appellation is distinctive and comforting. For
aperitif drinking.

8 Sainsbury's Classic Selection Sancerre 2004 £8.99
Bracing Sauvignon from the great AC of the Loire is very
firmly fruity and will match saucy fish dishes
magnificently.

GERMANY

8 Dr L Riesling 2004   £5.99
Appley, ethereal moselle of mild manners (only 8%
alcohol) and stimulating freshness.

ITALY

**8 Sainsbury's Classic Selection Pinot Grigio
2004**   £7.49
Perpetual in its popularity, PG is nevertheless mostly dull
stuff. Here's a better one, priced accordingly, with an
almost-bracing crispness to its green fruit and smoky,
spicy notes.

WHITE WINES	£5 PLUS

NEW ZEALAND

♈9 Sanctuary Pinot Gris 2004 £5.99
Lovely smoky cool-fruit off-dry exotic refresher of stimulating quality. In effect, Kiwi Pinot Grigio – and a major improvement on the Italian model in this price range.

♈9 Stoneleigh Sauvignon Blanc 2004 £6.99
Brisk, nettley style to a powerfully fruity dry wine in the classic Kiwi Sauvignon manner. Great value. Screwcap.

♈9 Jackson Estate Sauvignon Blanc 2004 £8.99
Benchmark quality from this asparagus-perfumed, grassy green and wonderfully vivid wine.

SOUTH AFRICA

♈8 Springfield Estate Special Cuvée
Sauvignon Blanc 2004 £7.49
Vivid green-grass, gooseberry style and refreshing character.

SPARKLING WINES	£5 PLUS

ENGLAND

Y8 **Chapel Down Century Bottle Fermented Dry** £11.99

The wordy name is by way of explaining this has been made by the 'champagne method', but the Champagne industry dislikes the use of the term by any but its own. I liked this wine's eager fizz, brioche nose and full fruit – all quite like 'real' Champagne. It's not extra dry; as the back label asserts, it's 'created with sweeter palates in mind'.

FRANCE

Y8 **Moët & Chandon Nectar Impérial Sec** £23.99

This isn't your standard Moët Imperial Brut, but a sweeter version with 'aromas of peach, apricot and barley sugar'. I thought it deliciously fruity and fun and not at all sugary.

Somerfield

There are major changes planned to the Somerfield wine range, so besides a few perennials that are almost certain to survive the axe of rationalisation, this is a much shorter listing than I would really like it to be.

But these stores are always worth a visit in the quest for good flavours and ever-changing bargains. Somerfield has a perpetual programme of wine discounts, but take note that the company expects customers to use its Saver Card to qualify for the money off.

'Saver Cards are readily and easily available from all Somerfield stores,' we are assured. 'Customers are not obliged to fill in any forms to pick up a card, and therefore qualify for the promotional prices on the wines. However, by completing the short, simple application form they will qualify for additional savings and offers on their shopping habits. So regular wine buyers will benefit from tailored wine offers and other deals relevant to them.'

RED WINES   UNDER £5

CHILE

9   Cono Sur Pinot Noir 2004   **£4.99**
The colour of this perennial classic is extraordinary – it's
pale as Pinot Noir reds so often are, but the ruby hue is
already taking on a hint of orange, as if this were a much
more mature wine. Lovely cherry whiff, a light quaffer
(though 13.5% alcohol) with juicy, enduring, refreshing
summer-fruit flavour. A true bargain.

ITALY

9   Serristori Sangiovese Merlot 2003   **£4.99**
A delightful juicy red from Umbria from Sangiovese, the
grape of Chianti, blended with the black-cherry evoking
Merlot. The painted decoration on the bottle is a bit naff,
but the wine is wonderfully lively, lush and complete. A
snip at this price.

USA

9   Leaping Horse Merlot 2002   **£4.99**
I think the name is unhelpful, but this beautifully
balanced sweet-cherry-fruit, firmly dry middleweight
Californian is an outright winner. Pure and simply
delicious.

RED WINES   £5 PLUS

S AFRICA

**8   Somerfield South African Limited Release
Shiraz 2004**   **£5.99**
Nice gripping plump red with satisfying dry rim to the
fruit. Screwcap.

SPAIN

8   Somerfield Viña Caña Rioja Reserva 2000   £6.99
Smells of old-fashioned garden roses and vanilla from
this light but elegantly flavoursome mature classic Rioja
at an unusually reasonable price.

PINK WINES — £5 PLUS

USA

⏻8 E&J Gallo Turning Leaf Syrah Rosé 2004 £5.99
Well-presented mega-brand has magenta colour and plenty of summer-fruit flavour. I do agree with the maker's claim that cranberry features here. So does barley sugar: just a hint of it before you get to the clean finish. Really a rather good, gutsy pink, with 13.5% alcohol and a screwcap.

WHITE WINES — UNDER £5

AUSTRALIA

⏻8 Tortoiseshell Bay Semillon Sauvignon 2004 £3.99
Scent of fresh pineapple and peach-melon fleshy flavours, all amounting to a lot of fun and flavour for the price.

SOUTH AFRICA

⏻8 Danie de Wet Chardonnay Sur Lie 2005 £4.49
Keen-edged bargain with stony-fresh fruit and a keen price, too.

USA

⏻8 Leaping Horse Chardonnay 2003 £4.99
Richly coloured with corresponding fruit balanced by edgy citrus acidity – very good fish wine.

White Wines   £5 Plus

AUSTRALIA

🍷9 **Jacob's Creek Reserve Chardonnay 2003**   £7.99
There's no getting away from it. This is a big brand name, perhaps the biggest, but it is fabulous wine, a masterly marriage of luxury fruit with mineral, citrus acidity. Tastes like a very expensive wine indeed.

NEW ZEALAND

🍷9 **Oyster Bay Sauvignon Blanc 2004**   £6.99
Famed dry white is typically zesty with a distinctive whiff of grapefruit and concentrated flavours including asparagus and gooseberry, even a hint of kiwi fruit! Screwcap.

Tesco

Britain's biggest retailer sells more than a fifth of all the wine we drink at home. Much of it is accounted for by the usual brands and discounted ranges, but it is an awful lot of wine, and makes Tesco the most powerful player in the business.

With 800 wines on its list, Tesco might be expected to take up a lot of space in this book, but this is not the case. I have not been invited to taste the range, and my requests for information have been stonewalled. That's power for you.

The few wines mentioned below are those I have bought – rather reluctantly, in light of head office's refusal to answer my calls and emails – from the stores.

RED WINES — UNDER £5

CHILE

▼9 **Cono Sur Pinot Noir 2004** £4.99
The colour of this perennial classic is extraordinary – it's pale as Pinot Noir reds so often are, but the ruby hue is already taking on a hint of orange, as if this were a much more mature wine. Lovely cherry whiff, a light quaffer (though 13.5% alcohol) with juicy, enduring, refreshing summer-fruit flavour. Fantastic bargain.

RED WINES — £5 PLUS

CHILE

▼9 **Casillero del Diablo Cabernet Sauvignon 2004** £5.49
Firm, blackcurranty Cabernet has generous weight, oaky velvet and stirring hint of spice. Seems cheap.

▼9 **Coteau Brulé Cairanne 2003** £5.99
Superior Côtes du Rhône Villages is smartly presented and entirely lives up to its promise. It's dark, dense and spicy in the proper manner, with a baked centre to the flavour in keeping with the brand name Coteau Brulé (burnt hillside). Cairanne is one of the villages within the appellation allowed to append its own name to its wines.

FRANCE

▼8 **Blason de Bourgogne Mercurey 2002** £9.98
Pale but handsome ruby colour and an intriguing peppery nose on this healthy, strawberry-fruit burgundy with clean, lipsmacking finish.

SOUTH AFRICA

▼9 **Thandi Pinot Noir 2002** £7.99
Fine mellow raspberry- and cherry-fruit silky red is a Fairtrade wine, which is admirable (it means the people in the Stellenbosch who make it enjoy fair pay and conditions), but the wine is also commendable entirely for itself. The name Thandi means nourishing love in Xhosa.

RED WINES   £5 PLUS

SPAIN

♥7 Las Postas Reserva Rioja 1999   £5.99
Mature, lightweight, goodish example with mellow
vanilla style.

♥8 Durius Tempranillo, Arribes del Duero
2003   £6.99
Lush, dark flavours with vanilla oakiness and spiky
highlights in this popular branded red. Very satisfying
indeed.

WHITE WINES   UNDER £5

GERMANY

♥7 St Johanner Abtey Spätlese 2004   £3.99
Verging on spritzy, this is arguably closer in style to an
apple drink than it is to Rhine wine. Some will like its
soft appeal, and there's just 10% alcohol.

SPAIN

♥9 Viña Sol 2004   £4.68
I hear this brilliant dry white from Miguel Torres in
Catalonia is becoming *de rigueur* in metropolitan 'style
bars'. And about time, too. It's one of the first branded
wines ever launched – back in the 1950s – and has been
consistently fresh, packed with green but lush fruit for all
the decades I've known it. On sale in most supermarkets.
Screwcap.

WHITE WINES	£5 PLUS

FRANCE

🍷**7** **Tesco Finest Alsace Gewürztraminer 2004** **£6.99**
Elegantly 'packaged' Gewürz is neatly poised between spicy richness and cleansing acidity. Not too much residual sugar (a common fault) but quite expensive.

NEW ZEALAND

🍷**9** **Montana East Coast
Unoaked Chardonnay 2004** **£5.56**
Although by far the biggest wine producer in New Zealand – the British-owned outfit is said to make more than half the total – Montana seems to turn out better and better products. This is their 'basic' Chardonnay and a lavishly delicious one, too, with glowing colour, pure sunny fruit and the clean minerality that is so much the Kiwi hallmark.

🍷**10** **Tesco Finest Marlborough
Sauvignon Blanc 2004** **£7.49**
Another brilliant vintage to succeed the top-scoring 2003, this is scintillating stuff. Packed with classic nettley-grassy Sauvignon fruit and tongue-tinglingly crisp and fresh. A match for big brands at much higher prices.

—Waitrose—

At their tastings for scribblers like me, Waitrose routinely line up more than 200 different wines – something like a third of the total range they sell. It's a generous gesture, and very much more so than any other supermarket chain.

I mention this partly by way of explaining why there are so many Waitrose wines in this book. Simple, really. I have tasted more wines from Waitrose than from any other retailer. But there is also the not-insignificant fact that a very high proportion of Waitrose wines are seriously good. No other supermarket comes within a country mile.

Particular strengths include lesser-known regions of France, a uniquely brilliant range from Germany, the best own-label sherries anywhere and a reassuringly small amount of space wasted on ubiquitous mega-brands. Prices are keen.

There is a widespread (though unsubstantiated) notion that Waitrose is more expensive than other supermarkets. As far as the wines are concerned, this is simply not true.

The stores themselves are now more widespread than they used to be, with new branches opening in the last year or so in northern counties. None in Scotland yet, but you can buy changing selections of the wines, and whole cases of all 600 on the list, online at **www.waitrose.com**.

ARGENTINA

8 Santa Julia FuZion Shiraz/Malbec 2003   £3.99
Gimmicky packaging, but a friendly, generous meat-dish matcher from an excellent producer, La Agricola.

AUSTRALIA

9 Palandri Pinnacle Shiraz 2002   £4.99
What's scarcer than emu's teeth? Drinkable Aussie wines under a fiver. But here's one, with rich but not overdone fruit and a long, pleasantly peppery tail.

BULGARIA

8 Sapphire Cove   £2.99
There's very little wine from Bulgaria in supermarkets these days, and this budget bottle is a welcome rarity. Mostly Merlot, with good dark colour, and well-defined brambly style.

CHILE

9 Cono Sur Pinot Noir 2004   £4.99
The colour of this perennial classic is extraordinary – it's pale as Pinot Noir reds so often are, but the ruby hue is already taking on a hint of orange, as if this were a much more mature wine. Lovely cherry whiff, a light quaffer (though 13.5% alcohol) with juicy, enduring, refreshing summer-fruit flavour. Fantastic bargain.

FRANCE

8 Cuvée Chasseur 2004   £3.05
Bargain vin de pays de l'Hérault is a ripe-smelling lightweight with spice and grip.

8 Corbières Domaine de la Perrière 2004   £3.99
Hot-climate red with tannic edge has endearing black-fruit flavours with soft, sweet centre.

RED WINES   UNDER £5

9 **Rue de France Rouge 2004**   £3.99
Pedestrian name does little justice to this lovable vin de
pays of the Vaucluse. It's quite light in body, but with
convincingly concentrated flavours and a refreshing edge.

10 **Saumur Les Nivières 2003**   £4.55
I swear this Loire wine gets better with every vintage. It
has the classic redcurrants and crushed leaves aroma of
the Cabernet Franc grape and firm but by no means
austere plummy flavour, finishing very clean. Highly
distinctive and a great match for lighter foods.

9 **Saint Roche, Vin de Pays des Bouches**
     du Rhône, 2004   £4.99
A gutsy deep-purple sunshine wine from Provence with
intriguing asparagus note in the flavour will be a good
winter-food matcher. Very likeable indeed.

8 **Waitrose Chianti 2003**   £3.99
Clean, bright cherry-fruit style is recognisably that of the
famous Tuscan wine.

7 **Inycon Shiraz 2003**   £4.99
Inycon, a brand of Sicily's biggest co-operative producer,
is improving. This one is ripe and not overcooked.

7 **The Cork Grove Castelao-Syrah 2003**   £4.49
Eager lightweight redcurranty glugger from Ribatejo
region has interesting gamey ripeness.

FRANCE

ITALY

PORTUGAL

RED WINES   UNDER £5

SPAIN

9 **Bodegas Innurieta Merlot NV 3-litre box** £14.99
The equivalent per-bottle price of this excellent Navarra red is £3.75, for which you get a perky, brambly, well-concentrated glugger with black-cherry ripeness and 14% alcohol. Unusually good quality from this kind of package.

USA

9 **Leaping Horse Vineyards Shiraz 2003** £4.99
I happened on this Californian marvel last year for the first time, and can continue confidently to back it in this vintage. Charming soft but tastebud-grabbing dry middleweight of real character, and a bargain.

RED WINES   £5 PLUS

ARGENTINA

8 **Finca Flichman Shiraz Reserva 2004** £5.99
Tannic gripper with 14.5% alcohol has spice and intensity. Firm but friendly.

AUSTRALIA

9 **Brown Brothers Tarrango 2003** £5.99
Pale-looking crisp red has lovely definition of flavour in a red-berry, keenly-edged style. Super summer slurper. Screwcap.

8 **Rutherglen Estates Durif 2004** £6.99
Distinctive black-fruit flavour of the Durif grape is a welcome contribution to Australian diversity. This is a likeable spicy red with 14.5% alcohol. Screwcap.

8 **Pirie South Pinot Noir 2004** £7.99
Tasmanian light-coloured Pinot has sweet cherry fruit.

RED WINES   £5 PLUS

**8 Wolf Blass President's Selection Cabernet
Sauvignon 2002   £11.99**
Flagship wine from a famed producer is worthy of the
name. Lavish, lingering new-oak style with a tidy finish
and 14.5% alcohol.

**9 Henschke Henry's Seven Shiraz/Grenache/
Viognier 2003   £14.99**
Henschke is one of the legends of the Barossa, whose
wines are not much seen in supermarkets. This is
perfection, lush and spicy and perfectly weighted (though
note 15% alcohol) and with what I can only call poised
elegance. Manna to Aussie wine fanatics.

**9 Casillero del Diablo Cabernet
Sauvignon 2004   £5.49**
Firm, blackcurranty Cabernet has generous weight, oaky
velvet and stirring hint of spice. Seems cheap.

**9 Gracia Merlot/Mourvèdre Reserva
Superior 2003   £5.99**
Part of the blend for this wine is 'aged in French Demptos
and Taransaud medium-toast barrels' and this might just
explain the very appealing creamy-silky black-cherry
style.

9 La Baume Selection Shiraz-Cabernet 2001 £6.99
Opaque monster vin de pays d'Oc (14.5% alcohol) from
hot and now maturing 2001 vintage has lavish minty
aroma and buckets of meaty, velvety black fruit.
Sumptuous.

AUSTRALIA

CHILE

FRANCE

Waitrose

FRANCE

**8 St-Chinian Cuvée des Fées,
Château Cazal Viel, 2003**   £6.99
The Château Cazal Viel wine estate in the Languedoc
belonged to the local monastery until the outbreak of the
French Revolution in 1789 when it was seized by the
family who still own it today. Contemplate this fact while
savouring the dense, spicy fruit and heavenly highlights
of violets in this venerable wine.

**10 Saumur-Champigny Les Tuffeaux,
Château de Targé, 2003**   £7.55
Fruit bomb from the Loire has real Cabernet Franc
character, with ripeness and a crunchy edge to the fruit.
Good food wine, to match tricky items like asparagus or
salads.

**9 Château La Varière, Cuvée Jacques
Beaujeau, 2003**   £7.99
A rather grand red from an obscure Loire Valley
appellation, Anjou-Villages Brissac, this is a discovery:
dark, rounded Cabernet Franc flavours with density and
structure.

9 Château Segonzac 2002   £7.99
Nice Côtes de Blaye claret with dense purple colour,
plump fruit and a tannic but friendly edge to the flavour.
This is a new-style 'fruit-driven' Bordeaux to drink now,
and even closed with a screwcap.

8 Juliénas, Georges Duboeuf, 2004   £7.99
After the lovely 2003 vintage for Beaujolais, it's a relief to
find something good from the less-auspicious 2004 –
evidence that the previous year might have been more than
a flash in the pan. This one has recognisable juicy, squishy
red fruit but some guts and structure too. Screwcap.

RED WINES   £5 PLUS

8 Château La Fleur Chambeau 2003   £8.49
Very dense and dark claret from satellite AC Lussac-St-Emilion has 14% alcohol and should evolve nicely. Drink from 2008.

9 Alsace Pinot Noir, Paul Blanck, 2004   £8.99
Alsatian red burgundy? It's utterly distinctive, with a sort of mineral purity, jumping with summer-ripe fruit, and a rare treat.

8 Chorey-lès-Beaune, Domaine Pascal
Maillard, 2003   £11.99
Alluring village burgundy has sweet, bloomy nose and lots of friendly strawberry fruit. Grand wine, but approachable.

9 Gigondas Les Espalines, Cuvée des
Tendrelles, 2003   £12.99
The Côtes du Rhône village of Gigondas produces a distinctly mixed bunch of wines under its own AC, but this is a very, very good one actually worth the money. It's ripe (14.5% alcohol), plump and spicy with a firm but friendly grip of tannin and will no doubt develop for years.

9 Corbières La Forge, Gérard Bertrand,
2001   £21.99
The AC of Corbières, west of Narbonne, enjoys a good name for spicy, occasionally tough, reds of yeoman character. But this one is an aristo – a big smoothie aged in new oak barrels to give it silk and richness and yet possessed of structured fruit flavours offering much to contemplate. Big wine (14% alcohol) of rare character to drink now or keep more or less indefinitely to await developments. Worth the money, honestly.

FRANCE

RED WINES	£5 PLUS

FRANCE

8 Gevrey-Chambertin Les Evocelles,
Domaine de la Vougeraie, 2003 £30.00
Grown-up wine, this is pure, lush Pinot Noir of great quality that's a treat now, but will improve for up to five years. Better than many others I've tasted, even in this price range.

ITALY

10 Vino Nobile di Montepulciano,
Carbonaia, 2001 £9.99
This great wine actually looks as rich and smooth as it tastes, with sleek, minty-violet-plum aromas and flavours. True luxury style with proper nutskin-dry finish in the Italian manner. A bit of a bargain by the standards of this famed and often pricy DOCG.

8 Amarone della Valpolicella Classico,
Vignale, 2001 £13.99
This specialist wine is made with grapes dried out for several months to concentrate their juice, and the effect is a dry but rich red with a liquorice kick (amarone means 'bitter') and a hefty 15% alcohol.

8 Brunello di Montalcino Tenuta Nuova,
Casanova de Neri, 2000 £20.00
Some of the red wines made from Brunello grapes grown around the Tuscan hilltown of Montalcino are among Italy's most ludicrously overpriced. Here's an honourable exception that's mature and authentically delicious.

RED WINES   £5 PLUS

9 **Montana Merlot/Cabernet 2003**   £6.99

Kiwi claret? Well, it's made from the same grape varieties
employed in Bordeaux. But the effect here is distinctly
different. You get a cool mintiness amid the blackcurrant
fruit, and intensity of colour and flavour entirely unlike
claret. Try it.

10 **Stoneleigh Pinot Noir 2003**   £7.99

Perfect strawberry-fruit Pinot is poised between
sweetness and purifying dryness. This is keenly priced for
such elevated quality, and I believe is a benchmark for
one of the world's great wine styles. Screwcap.

9 **Wither Hills Pinot Noir 2003**   £14.99

Probably the best Kiwi Pinot I've tasted in the year, but
rather expensive. Pure silk, with textbook NZ minty-
slinkiness and an awesome complexity. Screwcap.

8 **Jose de Sousa, JM Fonseca, 2001**   £5.99

Rustic minty-eucalyptus black-fruit classic Portuguese
red from the Alentejo region.

8 **Manta Preta 2003**   £5.99

Clove and cinnamon figure in the flavour mix of this
vanilla-rich and plumply fruity red from Estremadura
region.

8 **Esporao Reserva 2001**   £8.99

Bumper red from Alentejo region is jam-packed with
spicy, rich fruit, and 15% alcohol.

SOUTH AFRICA

9   **Diemersfontein Pinotage 2004**   £6.99

Toast and tar are among the evocations I scribbled in the note on this highly individual wine from the Cape's native Pinotage grape. It's dark and juicy and 14% alcohol, and would be ideal, I also noted, with shepherd's pie.

8   **Spice Route Pinotage 2003**   £7.99

Sweetly ripe but balanced red with a nice baked flavour in the middle. Very quaffable, but note 15% alcohol.

8   **The Chocolate Block 2003**   £14.99

In case you're tempted by the name, this won't disappoint. Huge dark spicy mature-tasting red with 15% alcohol and, yes, a distinct bitter-chocolate note in the depths of the flavour.

7   **Kumala Journey's End Shiraz 2003**   £14.99

Kumala is among the brands that have spearheaded South Africa's surge in the UK – this year reaching 10 per cent of the total in take-home sales. I'm not wild about the basic wines but this oaked luxury-end blackberry fruit bomb is pretty good, if pricy. It's 14% alcohol and needs a couple more years in the bottle to round out a bit.

SPAIN

8   **Gran Feudo Reserva Navarra 2000**   £6.55

Balanced, hedgerow-fruit red from Navarra region, neighbour to Rioja, has vigorous liveliness of flavour.

9   **Mas Collet, Celler de Capçanes, 2002**   £6.55

Consistently good Catalan red has deep and satisfying darkly spicy flavours all the way through from first sensation on the tongue to the lingering aftertaste.

RED WINES   £5 PLUS

SPAIN

9   **Toro Finca Sobreño Crianza 2001**   **£6.99**
Eye-catching orange label gives well-deserved shelf prominence to this black-as-night, chocolatey and velvety heavyweight (14% alcohol) from the fast-improving Toro region of Castille.

USA

9   **Bonterra Merlot 2002**   **£9.99**
Organic, shimmeringly pure and juicy black-cherry Californian with depth and plenty of grip (and 14% alcohol). Hate the outdated flange-topped bottle, but love the wine.

PINK WINES   UNDER £5

CHILE

8   **Mont Gras Zinfandel Rosé 2005**   **£4.99**
Magenta in colour and rather sweet, but not out of balance, this will please those who don't like their wine too dry.

FRANCE

8   **Waitrose Rosé d'Anjou 2004**   **£3.99**
Bog-standard Loire rosé is brisk, clean and balanced with a bit of underlying sweetness. Does the job.

ITALY

7   **Rosato Veronese, Cantina di
Monteforte, 2004**   **£4.15**
Delicate rose-petal smell and matching floral style to the fruit. Pale in colour, but plenty of interest.

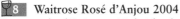

| PINK WINES | £5 PLUS |

CHILE

🍷10 **Torres San Medin Cabernet Sauvignon Rosé 2004**   £5.49
My top rosé of the year, and a bargain at this price. Bright, shocking pink colour, lush cassis nose and pure, crisp, lasting fruit flavours and 13.8% alcohol.

FRANCE

🍷8 **Domaine de Pellehaut Rosé 2004**   £5.15
Pleasing coral colour and floral whiff to this Gascon vin de pays, followed up by fresh, lightweight summer fruit.

NEW ZEALAND

🍷9 **Stoneleigh Pinot Noir Rosé 2004**   £6.99
The first Kiwi rosé I have tasted, and a flying start. Colour is nearer red than pink, and it has the typical cherry aroma of Pinot. Lively, full of summer fruit and delicious.

SPAIN

🍷8 **Muga Rosado Rioja 2004**   £5.99
Pale onion-skin in colour, this does actually taste like pink Rioja, and as such is pleasing and interesting.

| WHITE WINES | UNDER £5 |

ARGENTINA

🍷8 **Finca Las Higueras Pinot Gris 2004**   £4.99
Argentine Pinot Grigio, in effect, and an improvement on most of the Italian models, especially in this price range. Soft, generous style.

| WHITE WINES | UNDER £5 |

CHILE

8 Waitrose Chilean Chardonnay/Sauvignon
Blanc 2003 £4.49
Blend-for-all-tastes dry white is artfully balanced between the influences of the world's two favourite white grapes.

8 Cono Sur Limited Release Viognier 2004 £4.99
Soft but not flabby preserved-fruit flavours with a nice blanched-almond finish.

FRANCE

8 Cuvée Pêcheur 2004 £3.49
Very low price for this workmanlike, vegetal-smelling refresher from Toulouse.

8 Domaine de Planterieu 2004 £3.99
Gascon vin de pays is tingly fresh with lemon rim to the clean, grassy fruit.

9 Pujalet, Vin de Pays du Gers, 2004 £3.99
Sweet, floral smell, fleshy ripe orchard fruit and crisp-apple finish on this excitingly good bargain. Screwcap.

7 Waitrose Muscadet de Sèvre et Maine 2004 £3.99
Goodish example of the often fiercely acidic but enduringly popular dry white of the Loire estuary, this does have some appreciable racy fruitiness as well as the hallmark briny edge. Screwcap.

8 Saint-Pourçain Réserve Spéciale 2004 £4.75
Grassy green-fruit Loire bone-dry white has austere appeal. Good with mussels.

WHITE WINES	UNDER £5

FRANCE

8 **Muscadet Côtes de Grandlieu Sur Lie,
Fief Guérin, 2004** £4.99
Manageable salty tang to this quite-generously flavour-some variation on the theme. If you must drink Muscadet, drink this.

HUNGARY

7 **Chapel Hill Pinot Grigio 2002** £3.99
Pretty good by prevailing PG standards, a water-white but agreeably perfumed fresh style, keenly priced.

8 **Nagyréde Estate Chardonnay 2004** £3.99
Good colour and notes of peach, pear and even apricot in this rather exotic bargain. Screwcap.

8 **Riverview Sauvignon Blanc 2004** £3.99
Plenty of crispness and zing in this emphatic Sauvignon. It tastes as it ought to.

8 **Vignale Pinot Grigio 2004** £3.99
Popular style, this time with a bit of real fruit in it. Screwcap.

ITALY

8 **Gavi La Luciana, Araldica, 2004** £4.99
It creeps up on you, this one. Aromatic dry white with pleasingly vegetal flavours and a fine cutting edge.

8 **Italia Pinot Grigio 2004** £4.99
Crisp pear note somewhere in this dry but long-flavoured item. Clean finish. Screwcap.

MOLDOVA

8 **Firebird Legend Pinot Grigio 2003** £4.99
Lots of colour and an interesting mineral quality to the fruit salad of flavours.

WHITE WINES	£5 PLUS

ARGENTINA

🍷 **10** Catena Chardonnay 2003 £9.99

Enduring favourite with a superbly rich and ripe apple-pie fruit perfectly trimmed up with lime-trace acidity. Unmistakably special, vintage after vintage.

AUSTRALIA

🍷 **8** Leeuwin Estate Art Series Riesling 2004 £13.99

The frog label is fun, and the wine is remarkable, limey and complex, rather in the Alsace Riesling style. For enthusiasts of the genre.

AUSTRIA

🍷 **8** Gobelsburger Grüner Veltliner 2004 £5.99

This positively prickles with freshness and orchard flavours. An appley refresher to stimulate the appetite.

🍷 **8** Felsner Grüner Veltliner Moosburgerin Kabinett 2004 £7.99

Richly coloured, grapy dry white has mineral crispness, appley fruit and satisfying complexity. Really rather good as a stand-alone wine.

FRANCE

🍷 **9** Château Saint-Jean-des-Graves 2004 £5.99

Classic blend of Sauvignon and Sémillon makes for exotically perfumed, brightly stimulating grassy-tropical dry white of real elegance. Screwcap.

🍷 **9** Dourthe No 1 Sauvignon Blanc 2004 £5.99

Big brand Bordeaux dry white has sunny, pineappley nose and a nice balance of lushness and stony freshness. Class act, and it's refreshing in more ways than one to find such an excellent mass-produced wine from this troubled region. Screwcap.

Waitrose

FRANCE

8 **Gewürztraminer, Cave de Turckheim, 2004 £6.99**
Supermarket Alsace Gewürz can be pretty dismal but this one is bright and fresh as well as aromatic and spicy.

8 **Sauvignon Blanc, Vin de Pays de l'Yonne, 2004 £6.99**
A humble vin de pays maybe, but this is from the northern reaches of the Burgundy region, where they make stylish green-fruit Sauvignon of real distinction. This is grassy and limey with an assertive citrus finish.

9 **Sirius Bordeaux Blanc 2003 £6.99**
Yet another absolutely cracking white Bordeaux, this time with a nose I have described in my note as evoking buttery scrambled egg. A plush but crisply fresh dry white of serious interest.

9 **La Grille Classic Sauvignon Blanc, Henri Bourgeois, 2004 £7.49**
This is Sancerre (the smartest AC of the Loire) in all but name, and a lush, complete, herbaceous wine of patently obvious quality. Classified as a humble vin de pays du Jardin de la France, it's a great comfort for Sancerrophiles who don't like paying the usual £10-plus.

8 **Petit Chablis, Cave des Vignerons de Chablis, 2004 £7.99**
Do I detect the legendary 'gold shot with green' colour attributed to Chablis? The flavour is certainly well up to snuff, not 'petit' but quite plump and rich, with signature Chablis flintiness in the depths.

WHITE WINES   £5 PLUS

FRANCE

 8   **Pouilly-Vinzelles Les Longeays,
Domaine Thibert, 2003**   **£8.99**
Gold colour, extravagant near-spirity scent with a whiff
of brassica, and rich-but-restrained Chardonnay fruit.

 9   **Meursault Le Limozin,
Vincent Girardan, 2002**   **£19.99**
Convincing rebuttal of snobbish wine-trade notion that
you can't buy good burgundy in a supermarket. This
one's the business, with sumptuous yellow fruit and
perfect mineral balance. Tastes very expensive.

9   **The Naked Grape Riesling 2004**   **£5.99**
Gimmicky presentation doesn't spoil this outstanding dry
wine from the Palatinate, made by the great Ernie
Loosen. Apple-crisp, long-flavoured racy style. Screwcap.

10   **Hattenheimer Wisselbrunnen Riesling
Spätlese, Von Simmern, 2002**   **£9.95**
Colour is going gold and there is already a hint of petrol
in the nose of this dry but honeyed classic from a great
Rheingau producer. Lovely now and for the future, it has
10% alcohol.

GERMANY

9   **Rüdesheimer Berg Rottland Riesling
Spätlese, Dr Wegler, 2002**   **£9.95**
Yet another great classic, this time from a top Mosel
producer, has a keen-edged, fabulously racy fruit with
intense, lingering flavours. Superb wine with 8% alcohol.

9   **Scharzhofberger Riesling Spätlese,
Von Hövel, 2004**   **£9.99**
From one of the great vineyards of the Saar valley, a
delicately rich, floral, honey-hinting wine of great
character. Just 7% alcohol.

WHITE WINES   £5 PLUS

ITALY

8 **Lugana Villa Flora, Zenato, 2004**   £5.99
Perennial Lake Garda favourite is as fresh and intriguing as ever, with appealing colour and long, ripe fruit flavours.

NEW ZEALAND

9 **Stoneleigh Sauvignon Blanc 2004**   £6.99
Brisk, nettley style to a powerfully fruity dry wine in the classic Kiwi Sauvignon manner. Great value. Screwcap.

9 **Villa Maria Private Bin Gewürztraminer**
2004   £8.05
Fascinating lychee-perfumed, exotically rich, spicy and smoky dry white closely resembles the classic Alsace style, and may even improve on it. Thrilling stuff, wearing its 14% alcohol lightly.

PORTUGAL

7 **Quinta de Simaens Vinho Verde 2004**   £5.49
At the height of vinho verde's popularity, most of it was dull, sweetened stuff, but this survivor is better than that – fresh and crisp, if by no means 'green'.

8 **Borges Alvarinho Vinho Verde 2004**   £8.99
Layered flavours in this zesty invigorator make for distinctive refreshment.

SOUTH AFRICA

8 **Porcupine Ridge Sauvignon Blanc 2004**   £5.99
Sweet-smelling floral crowd-pleaser is consistent and fresh. Screwcap.

9 **Bouchard Finlayson Crocodile's Lair**
Chardonnay 2003   £9.99
Snappy name it's not, but a lush, toothsome dry white of well-balanced concentration and crispness. Lavish, lingering and 14% alcohol.

WHITE WINES	£5 PLUS

S AFRICA

♟8 Rustenberg Chardonnay 2003　　　£9.99
Tangy-toasty balance of lemony freshness and
extravagant ripeness, with 14.5% alcohol.

SPAIN

♟8 Palacio des Bornos Verdejo Rueda 2004　£5.99
Melon fruit in this ripe and sunny dry white from
excellent Rueda region.

♟9 Cune Monopole Rioja Blanco 2003　　£6.49
High mark for this white Rioja because of its
unreconstructed style. It's gold in colour, has a sweet
vanilla nose and seductive ripeness, but it's beautifully
made, with vivid freshness and a keen edge.

USA

♟9 Bonterra Chardonnay 2002　　　　£8.99
Opulent straw colour to this organic Californian, which
balances luxurious richness with keen flavours
embracing apples, asparagus, even spinach.

SPARKLING WINES	£5 PLUS

ENGLAND

9 **Ridgeview Bloomsbury Cuvée Merret 2001** £14.99
Very well contrived pretender to the Champagne style from West Sussex. Good fun for patriotic occasions, and a lovely sparkler in its own right.

8 **Nyetimber Blanc de Blancs 1996** £19.00
Mature sparkler with fine gold colour and a nice hint of brioche. Very like Champagne, really.

FRANCE

8 **Sparkling White Burgundy** £7.99
Lots of crisp apple fruit in this vigorous sparkler from Chardonnay grapes – one of the mainstays of Champagne itself – cultivated in their indigenous region, Burgundy. I liked this much more than Australian and Californian counterparts at the same sort of price.

9 **Waitrose Blanc de Noirs Brut** £15.99
One of my favourite supermarket fizzes, this has crisp but creamy flavour and plenty of intensity. I'd call it rounded, even 'commercial', and at the price much better value than some of the big-name brands.

10 **Waitrose Brut Vintage 1996** £19.99
This is such a treat, benefiting greatly from its near-venerable age, and delivering layered, satisfying flavours through a vivacious, small-bubble fizz.

ITALY

7 **Prosecco La Marca** £5.99
Water-white, sweet-nosed, sappy but not unpleasant fruit and plenty of lively fizz. Prosecco is trendy, and not always as good even as this.

FORTIFIED WINES UNDER £5

SPAIN

 8 **Waitrose Fino Sherry** £4.75
Tangy but not sharp bone-dry pale sherry at just 15% alcohol, this is amazing value for drinking chilled and fresh.

FORTIFIED WINES £5 PLUS

PORTUGAL

8 **Warre's Otima 20-Year-old Tawny Port** £18.49
(50cl)
My first taste of this, and it's a worthy senior partner to the popular 10-year-old Otima Tawny. Fine copper colour, rich, creamy, minty, fruitcake complexity. Luxury wine at an appropriate price.

SPAIN

10 **Waitrose Solera Jerezano Dry**
Amontillado Sherry £6.55
Lovely tawny colour, and a perfect balance of fruit-and-nuttiness with keen freshness. Off-dry, excitingly complex and 19% alcohol. Top-quality sherry at a giveaway price.

What Wine Words Mean

Wine labels convey a lot of information, some of it useful. Under a combination of UK and EU regulations, the quantity and alcoholic strength of the contents must be displayed, as must the country of origin. And besides the wines from the traditional regions and appellations of France (Bordeaux, Burgundy, etc.), Italy (Barolo, Chianti) and Spain (Rioja, Navarra), the label is also very likely to bear the name of the grape or grapes involved. In the mass market, grape names such as Chardonnay and Shiraz now count for a lot more than this or that vineyard, region or even nation.

So, this glossary includes the names of more than 60 different grape varieties along with brief descriptions of their characteristics. The varietal name on a label tells you more than anything else about what to expect of the wine.

Other items in this vocabulary include short summaries of the regions and appellations of recommended wines and some of the many label designations given to the style, alleged quality and regulatory classifications.

Finally, I have tried to explain in simple and rational terms the many peculiar words I use in trying to convey the characteristics of wines described. 'Delicious' might need no further qualification, but the likes of 'bouncy', 'green' and 'liquorous' probably do.

A

abboccato – Medium-dry white wine style. Italy, especially Orvieto.

AC – See Appellation d'Origine Contrôlée.

acidity – To be any good, every wine must have the right level of acidity. It gives wine the element of dryness or sharpness it needs to prevent cloying sweetness or dull wateriness. If there is too much acidity, wine tastes raw or acetic (vinegary). Winemakers strive to create balanced acidity – either by cleverly controlling the natural processes, or by adding sugar and acid to correct imbalances.

aftertaste – The flavour that lingers in the mouth after swallowing the wine.

Aglianico – Black grape variety of southern Italy. It has romantic associations. When the ancient Greeks first colonised Italy in the seventh century BC, it was with the prime purpose of planting it as a vineyard (the Greek name for Italy was Oenotria – land of cultivated vines). The name for the vines the Greeks brought with them was Ellenico (as in Hellas, Greece), from which Aglianico is the modern rendering. To return to the point, these ancient vines, especially in the arid volcanic landscapes of Basilicata and Cilento, produce excellent dark, earthy and highly distinctive wines. A name to look out for.

Agriculture biologique – On French wine labels, an indication that the wine has been made by organic methods.

Albariño – White grape variety of Spain that makes intriguingly perfumed fresh and spicy dry wines, especially in the esteemed Rias Baixas region.

Almansa – DO winemaking region of Spain inland from Alicante, making great-value red wines.

alcohol – The alcohol levels in wines are expressed in terms of alcohol by volume ('abv'), that is, the percentage of the volume of the wine that is common, or ethyl, alcohol. A typical wine at 12 per cent abv is thus 12 parts alcohol and, in effect, 88 parts fruit juice.

The question of how much alcohol we can drink without harming ourselves in the short or long term is an impossible one to answer, but there is more or less general agreement among scientists that small amounts of alcohol are good for us, even if the only evidence of this is actuarial – the fact that mortality statistics show teetotallers live significantly shorter lives than moderate drinkers. According to the Department of Health, there are 'safe limits' to the amount of alcohol we should drink weekly. These limits are measured in units of alcohol, with a small glass of wine taken to be one unit. Men are advised that 28 units a week is the most they can drink without risk to health, and for women (whose liver function differs from men's because of metabolic variations) the figure is 21 units.

If you wish to measure your consumption closely, note that a standard 75 cl bottle of wine at 12 per cent alcohol contains nine units. A bottle of German Moselle at 8 per cent alcohol has only six units, but a bottle of Australian Chardonnay at 14 per cent has 10.5.

Alentejo – Wine region of southern Portugal (immediately north of the Algarve), with a fast-improving reputation, especially for sappy, keen reds from local grape varieties including Aragones, Castelão and Trincadeira grapes.

Alsace – France's easternmost wine-producing region lies between the Vosges Mountains and the River Rhine, with Germany beyond. These conditions make for the production of some of the world's most delicious and fascinating white wines, always sold under the name of their constituent grapes. Pinot Blanc is the most affordable – and is well worth looking out for. The 'noble' grape varieties of the region are

Gewürztraminer, Muscat, Riesling and Tokay Pinot Gris and they are always made on a single-variety basis. The richest, most exotic wines are those from individual grand cru vineyards, which are named on the label. Some vendange tardive (late harvest) wines are made, but tend to be expensive. All the wines are sold in tall, slim green bottles known as flûtes that closely resemble those of the Mosel, and the names of producers and grape varieties are often German too, so it is widely assumed that Alsace wines are German in style, if not in nationality. But this is not the case in either particular. Alsace wines are dry and quite unique in character – and definitely French.

Amarone – Style of red wine made in Valpolicella, Italy. Specially selected grapes are held back from the harvest and stored for several months to dry them out. They are then pressed and fermented into a highly concentrated speciality dry wine. Amarone means 'bitter', describing the dry style of the flavour.

amontillado – See Sherry.

aperitif – If a wine is thus described, I believe it will give more pleasure before a meal than with one. Crisp, low-alcohol German wines and other delicately flavoured whites (including many dry Italians) are examples.

Appellation d'Origine Contrôlée – Commonly abbreviated to AC or AOC, this is the system under which quality wines are defined in France. About a third of the country's vast annual output qualifies, and there are more than 400 distinct AC zones. The declaration of an AC on the label signifies that the wine meets standards concerning location of vineyards and wineries, grape varieties and limits on harvest per hectare, methods of cultivation and vinification, and alcohol content. Wines are inspected and tasted by state-appointed committees. The one major aspect of any given wine that an AC cannot guarantee is that you will like it – but it certainly improves the chances.

Apulia – Anglicised name for Puglia.

Ardèche – Region of southern France to the west of the Rhône valley, home to a good vin de pays zone known as the Coteaux de L'Ardèche. Lots of decent-value reds from Syrah grapes, and some, less interesting, dry whites.

Assyrtiko – White grape variety of Greece now commonly named on dry white wines, sometimes of great quality, from the mainland and islands.

Asti – Town and major winemaking centre in Piedmont, Italy. The sparkling (spumante) sweet wines made from Moscato grapes are inexpensive and often delicious. Typical alcohol level is a modest 5 to 7 per cent.

attack – In wine tasting, the first impression made by the wine in the mouth.

auslese – German wine-quality designation. See QmP.

B

backbone – A personal item of wine-tasting terminology. It's the impression given by a well-made wine in which the flavours are a pleasure to savour at all three stages: initial sensation in the mouth; while being held in the mouth; in the aftertaste when the wine has been swallowed or spat out. Such a wine is held together by backbone.

Baga – Black grape variety indigenous to Portugal. Makes famously concentrated, juicy reds that get their deep colour from the grape's particularly thick skins. Look out for this name, now quite frequently quoted as the varietal on Portuguese wine labels. Often very good value for money.

balance – A big word in the vocabulary of wine tasting. Respectable wine must get two key things right: lots of fruitiness from the sweet grape juice, and plenty of acidity so the sweetness is 'balanced' with the crispness familiar in good dry whites and the dryness that marks out good reds. Some wines are noticeably 'well balanced' in that they have memorable fruitiness and the clean, satisfying 'finish' (last flavour in the mouth) that ideal acidity imparts.

Barbera – Black grape variety originally of Piedmont in Italy. Most commonly seen as Barbera d'Asti, the vigorously fruity red wine made around Asti – which is better known for sweet sparkling Asti Spumante. Barbera grapes are now being grown in South America, often producing a sleeker, smoother style than at home in Italy.

Bardolino – Once-fashionable, light red wine DOC of Veneto, north-west Italy. Bardolino is made principally from Corvina Veronese grapes plus Rondinella, Molinara and Negrara. Best wines are supposed to be those labelled classico, and superiore is applied to those aged a year and having at least 11.5 per cent alcohol.

Barossa Valley – Famed vineyard region north of Adelaide, Australia, produces hearty reds principally from Shiraz, Cabernet Sauvignon and Grenache grapes, plus plenty of lush white wine from Chardonnay. Also known for limey, long-lived, mineral dry whites from Riesling grapes.

barrique – Barrel in French. 'En barrique' on a wine label signifies the wine has been matured in oak.

Beaujolais – Unique red wines from the southern reaches of Burgundy, France, are made from Gamay grapes. Beaujolais nouveau, the new wine of each harvest, is released on the third Thursday of every November to much ballyhoo. It provides a friendly introduction to this deliciously bouncy, fleshily fruity wine style. Decent Beaujolais for enjoying during the rest of the year has lately become rather more expensive. If splashing out, go for Beaujolais Villages, from the region's better, northern vineyards. There are ten AC zones within the northern part of the region making wines under their own names. Known as the 'crus', these are

Brouilly, Chénas, Chiroubles, Côte de Brouilly, Fleurie, Juliénas, Morgon, Moulin à Vent, Regnié and St Amour, and they produce most of the very best wines of the region – at prices a pound or two higher than for Beaujolais Villages.

Beaumes de Venise – Village near Châteauneuf du Pape in France's Rhône valley, famous for sweet and alcoholic wine from Muscat grapes. Delicious, grapey wines. A small number of growers also make strong (sometimes rather tough) red wines under the village name.

Beaune – One of the two winemaking centres (the other is Nuits St Georges) at the heart of Burgundy in France. Three of the region's humbler appellations take the name of the town: Côtes de Beaune, Côtes de Beaune Villages and Hautes Côtes de Beaune. Wines made under these ACs are often, but by no means always, good value for money.

berry fruit – Some red wines deliver a burst of flavour in the mouth that corresponds to biting into a newly picked berry – strawberry, blackberry, etc. So a wine described as having berry fruit (by this writer, anyway) has freshness, liveliness, immediate appeal.

bianco – White wine, Italy.

Bical – White grape variety principally of Dão region of northern Portugal. Not usually identified on labels, because most of it goes into inexpensive sparkling wines. Can make still wines of very refreshing crispness.

biodynamics – A cultivation method taking the organic approach several steps further. Biodynamic winemakers plant and tend their vineyards according to a date and time calendar 'in harmony' with the movements of the planets. Some of France's best-known wine estates subscribe, and many more are going that way. It might all sound bonkers, but it's salutary to learn that biodynamics is based on principles first described by a very eminent man, the Austrian educationist Rudolph Steiner. He's lately been in the news for having written, in 1919, that farmers crazy enough to feed animal products to cattle would drive their livestock 'mad'.

bite – In wine tasting, the impression on the palate of a wine with plenty of acidity and, often, tannin.

blanc – White wine, France.

blanc de blancs – White wine from white grapes, France. May seem to be stating the obvious, but some white wines (e.g. Champagne) are made, partially or entirely, from black grapes.

blanc de noirs – White wine from black grapes, France. Usually sparkling (especially Champagne), made from black Pinot Meunier and Pinot Noir grapes, with no Chardonnay or other white varieties.

blanco – White wine, Spain and Portugal.

Blauer Zweigelt – Black grape variety of Austria, making a large proportion of the country's red wines, some of excellent quality.

Bobal – Black grape variety mostly of southeastern Spain. Thick skin is good for colour and juice contributes acidity to blends.

bodega – In Spain, a wine producer or wine shop.

Bonarda – Black grape variety of northern Italy. Now more widely planted in Argentina, where it makes rather elegant red wines, often representing great value.

botrytis – Full name *botrytis cinerea*, is a beneficent fungus that can attack ripe grape bunches late in the season, shrivelling the berries to a gruesome-looking mess, which yields concentrated juice of prized sweetness. Cheerfully known as 'noble rot', this fungus is actively encouraged by winemakers in regions as diverse as Sauternes (in Bordeaux),

Monbazillac (in Bergerac), the Rhine and Mosel valleys and South Australia to make ambrosial dessert wines.

bouncy – The feel in the mouth of a red wine with young, juicy fruitiness. Good Beaujolais is bouncy as are many north-west Italian wines from Barbera and Dolcetto grapes.

Bourgogne Grand Ordinaire – Appellation of France's Burgundy region for 'ordinary' red wines from either Gamay or Pinot Noir grapes, or both. Some good-value wines, especially from the Buxy Co-operative in the southern Chalonnais area.

Bourgueil – Appellation of Loire Valley, France. Long-lived red wines from Cabernet Franc grapes.

briary – In wine-tasting, associated with the flavours of fruit from prickly bushes such as blackberries.

brûlé – Pleasant burnt-toffee taste or smell, as in crème brûlée.

brut – Driest style of sparkling wine. Originally French, for very dry Champagnes specially developed for the British market, but now used for sparkling wines from all round the world.

Buzet – Little-seen AC of south-west France overshadowed by Bordeaux but producing some characterful ripe reds.

C

Cabardès – New AC (1998) for red and rosé wines from area north of Carcassonne, Aude, France. Principally Cabernet Sauvignon and Merlot grapes.

Cabernet franc – Black grape variety originally of France. It makes the light-bodied and keenly-edged red wines of the Loire Valley – such as Chinon and Saumur. And it is much grown in Bordeaux, especially in the appellation of St Emilion. Also now planted in Argentina, Australia and North

America. Wines, especially in the Loire, are characterised by a leafy, sappy style and bold fruitiness. Most are best enjoyed young.

Cabernet Sauvignon – Black (or, rather, blue) grape variety now grown in virtually every wine-producing nation. When perfectly ripened, the grapes are smaller than many other varieties and have particularly thick skins. This means that, when pressed, Cabernet grapes have a high proportion of skin to juice – and that makes for wine with lots of colour and tannin. In Bordeaux, the grape's traditional home, the grandest Cabernet-based wines have always been known as vins de garde (wines to keep) because they take years, even decades, to evolve as the effect of all that skin extraction preserves the fruit all the way to magnificent maturity. But in today's impatient world, these grapes are exploited in modern winemaking techniques to produce the sublime flavours of mature Cabernet without having to hang around for lengthy periods awaiting maturation. While there's nothing like a fine, ten-year-old claret (and nothing quite as expensive), there are many excellent Cabernets from around the world that amply illustrate this grape's characteristics. Classic smells and flavours include blackcurrants, cedar wood, chocolate, tobacco – even violets.

Cahors – An AC of the Lot Valley in south-west France once famous for 'black wine'. This was a curious concoction of straightforward wine mixed with a soupy must, made by boiling up new-pressed juice to concentrate it (through evaporation) before fermentation. The myth is still perpetuated that Cahors wine continues to be made in this way, but production on this basis actually ceased 150 years ago. Cahors today is no stronger, or blacker, than the wines of neighbouring appellations.

Cairanne – Village of the appellation collectively known as the Côtes du Rhône Villages in south France. Cairanne is one of several villages entitled to put their name on the labels of wines made within their AC boundary, and the appearance of this name is quite reliably an indicator of a very good wine indeed.

Calatayud – DO (quality wine zone) near Zaragoza in the Aragon region of northern Spain where they're making some astonishingly good wines at bargain prices, mainly reds from Garnacha and Tempranillo grapes. These are the varieties that go into the light and oaky wines of Rioja, but in Calatayud the wines are dark, dense and decidedly different.

cantina sociale – See Co-op.

Carignan – Black grape variety of Mediterranean France. It is rarely identified on labels, but is a major constituent of wines from the southern Rhône and Languedoc-Roussillon regions, especially the cheaper brands. Known as Carignano in Italy and Cariñena in Spain.

Carmenère – Black grape variety once widely grown in Bordeaux but abandoned due to cultivation problems. Lately revived in South America where it is producing fine wines.

cassis – As a tasting note, signifies a wine has a noticeable blackcurrant-concentrate flavour or smell. Much associated with the Cabernet Sauvignon grape.

Castelao – Portuguese black grape variety. Same as Periquita.

Catarratto – White grape variety of Sicily. In skilled hands it can make anything from keen, green-fruit dry whites to lush, oaked super-ripe styles. Also used for marsala.

cat's pee – In tasting notes, a mildly jocular reference to a certain style of Sauvignon Blanc wine.

cava – The sparkling wine of Spain. Most originates in Catalonia, but the Denominacion de Origen (DO) guarantee of authenticity is open to producers in many regions of the country. Much cava is very reasonably priced even though it is made by the same method as Champagne – second fermentation in bottle, known in Spain as the metodo classico.

CdR – Côtes du Rhône.

Cépage – Grape variety, French. 'Cépage Merlot' on a label simply means the wine is made largely or exclusively from Merlot grapes.

Chablis – Northernmost AC of France's Burgundy region. Its dry white wines from Chardonnay grapes are known for their fresh and steely style, but the best wines also age very gracefully into complex classics.

Chambourcin – Sounds like a cream cheese but it's a relatively modern (1963) French hybrid black grape that makes some good non-appellation lightweight-but-concentrated reds in the Loire Valley and now some heftier versions in Australia.

Chardonnay – The world's most popular grape variety. Said to originate from the village of Chardonnay in the Mâconnais region of southern Burgundy, the vine is now planted in every wine-producing nation. Wines are commonly characterised by generous colour and sweet-apple smell, but styles range from lean and sharp to opulently rich. Australia started the craze for oaked Chardonnay, the gold-coloured, super-ripe, buttery 'upfront' wines that are a caricature of lavish and outrageously expensive Burgundies such as Meursault and Puligny-Montrachet. Rich to the point of egginess, these Aussie pretenders are now giving way to a sleeker, more minerally style with much less oak presence – if any at all. California and Chile, New Zealand and South Africa are competing hard to imitate the Burgundian style, and Australia's success in doing so.

Châteauneuf du Pape – Famed appellation centred on a picturesque village of the southern Rhône valley in France where in the 1320s French Pope Clement V had a splendid new château built for himself as a country retreat amidst his vineyards. The red wines of the AC, which can be made from 13 different grape varieties but principally Grenache, Syrah and Mourvèdre, are regarded as the best of the southern Rhône and have become rather expensive – but they can be sensationally good. Expensive white wines are also made.

Chenin blanc – White grape variety of the Loire Valley, France. Now also grown farther afield, especially in South Africa. Makes dry, soft white wines and also rich, sweet styles. Sadly, many low-cost Chenin wines are bland and uninteresting.

cherry – In wine-tasting, either a pale red colour or, more commonly, a smell or flavour akin to the sun-warmed, bursting sweet ripeness of cherries. Many Italian wines, from lightweights such as Bardolino and Valpolicella to serious Chianti, have this character. 'Black cherry' as a description is often used of Merlot wines – meaning they are sweet but have a firmness associated with the thicker skins of black cherries.

Cinsault – Black grape variety of southern France, where it is invariably blended with others in wines of all qualities ranging from vin de pays to the pricy reds of Châteauneuf du Pape. Also much-planted in South Africa. The effect in wine is to add keen aromas (sometimes compared with turpentine!) and softness to the blend. The name is often spelt Cinsaut.

Clape, La – A small cru (defined quality-vineyard area) within the Coteaux du Languedoc where the growers make some seriously delicious red wines, mainly from Carignan, Grenache and Syrah grapes. A name worth looking out for on labels from the region.

claret – The red wine of Bordeaux, France. It comes from Latin *clarus*, meaning 'clear', recalling a time when the red wines of the region were much lighter in colour than they are now.

clarete – On Spanish labels indicates a pale-coloured red wine. 'Tinto' signifies a deeper hue.

classed growth – English translation of French *cru classé* describes a group of 60 individual wine estates in the Médoc district of Bordeaux, which in 1855 were granted this new status on the basis that their wines were the most expensive at that time. The classification was a promotional wheeze to attract attention to the Bordeaux stand at that year's Great Exhibition in Paris. Amazingly, all of the 60 wines concerned are still in production and most still occupy more or less their original places in the pecking order price-wise. The league was divided up into five divisions from Premier Grand Cru Classé (just four wines originally, with one promoted in 1971 – the only change ever made to the classification) to Cinquième Grand Cru Classé. Other regions of Bordeaux, notably Graves and St Emilion, have since imitated Médoc and introduced their own rankings of cru classé estates.

classic – An overused term in every respect, wine descriptions being no exception. In this book, the word is used to describe a very good wine of its type. So, a 'classic' Cabernet Sauvignon is one that is recognisably and admirably characteristic of that grape.

Classico – Under Italy's wine laws, this word appended to the name of a DOC zone has an important significance. The classico wines of the region can only be made from vineyards lying in the best-rated areas, and wines thus labelled (e.g. Chianti Classico, Soave Classico, Valpolicella Classico) can be reliably counted on to be a cut above the rest.

Colombard – White grape variety of southern France. Once employed almost entirely for making the wine that is distilled for armagnac and cognac brandies, but lately restored to varietal prominence in the Vin de Pays des Côtes de Gascogne where high-tech wineries turn it into a fresh and crisp, if unchallenging, dry wine at a budget price. But beware, cheap Colombard (especially from South Africa) can still be very dull.

Conca de Barbera – Winemaking region of Catalonia, Spain.

co-op – Very many of France's good-quality, inexpensive wines are made by co-operatives. These are wine-producing factories whose members, and joint-owners, are local vignerons (vine-growers). Each year they sell their harvests to the co-op for turning into branded wines. In Italy, co-op wines can be identified by the words 'Cantina Sociale' on the label and in Germany by the term 'Winzergenossenschaft'.

Corbières – A name to look out for. It's an AC of France's Midi (deep south) and produces countless robust reds and a few interesting whites, often at bargain prices.

Cortese – White grape variety of Piedmont, Italy. At its best, makes amazingly delicious, keenly brisk and fascinating wines, including those of the Gavi DOCG. Worth seeking out.

Costières de Nîmes – Until 1989, this AC of southern France was known as the Costières de Gard. It forms a buffer between the southern Rhône and Languedoc-Roussillon regions, and makes wines from broadly the same range of grape varieties. It's a name to look out for, the best red wines being notable for their concentration of colour and fruit, with the earthy-spiciness of the better Rhone wines and a likeable liquorice note. A few good white wines, too, and even a decent rosé or two.

Côte – In French, it simply means a side, or slope, of a hill. The implication in wine terms is that the grapes come from a vineyard ideally situated for maximum sunlight, good drainage and the unique soil conditions prevailing on the hill in question. It's fair enough to claim that vines grown on slopes might get more sunlight than those grown on the flat, but there is no guarantee whatsoever that any wine labelled

'Côtes du' this or that is made from grapes grown on a hillside at all. Côtes du Rhône wines are a case in point. Many 'Côtes' wines come from entirely level vineyards and it is worth remembering that many of the vineyards of Bordeaux, producing most of the world's priciest wines, are little short of prairie-flat. The quality factor is determined much more significantly by the weather and the talents of the winemaker.

Côtes de Blaye – Appellation Contrôlée zone of Bordeaux on the right bank of the river Gironde, opposite the more prestigious Médoc zone of the left bank. A couple of centuries ago, Blaye (pronounced 'bligh') was the grander of the two, and even today makes some wines that compete well for quality, and at a fraction of the price of wines from its more fashionable rival across the water.

Côtes du Luberon – Appellation Contrôlée zone of Provence in south-east France. Wines, mostly red, are similar in style to Côtes du Rhône.

Côtes du Rhône – One of the biggest and best-known appellations of south-east France, covering an area roughly defined by the southern reaches of the valley of the River Rhône. Long notorious for cheap and execrable reds, the Côtes du Rhône AC has lately achieved remarkable improvements in quality at all points along the price scale. Lots of brilliant-value warm and spicy reds, principally from Grenache and Syrah grapes. There are also some white and rosé wines. Note that this region had a brilliant run of vintages up to 2001 but then a rain-and-storm-ruined one in 2002. Go for pre-2002 vintages if you have a choice.

Côtes du Rhône Villages – Appellation within the larger Côtes du Rhône AC for wine of supposed superiority made in a number of zones associated with a long list of nominated individual villages. Villages wines may be more interesting than their humbler counterparts, but this cannot be counted on. Go for the 2000 and 2001 vintages rather than 2002.

Côtes du Roussillon – Huge appellation of south-west France known for strong, dark, peppery reds often offering very decent value.

Côtes du Roussillon Villages – Appellation for superior wines from a number of nominated locations within the larger Roussillon AC. Some of these village wines can be of exceptional quality and value.

crianza – Means 'nursery' in Spanish. On Rioja and Navarra wines, the designation signifies a wine that has been nursed through a maturing period of at least a year in oak casks and a further six months in bottle before being released for sale.

cru – A word that crops up with confusing regularity on French wine labels. It means 'the growing' or 'the making' of a wine and asserts that the wine concerned is from a specific vineyard. Under the Appellation Contrôlée rules, countless crus are classified in various hierarchical ranks. Hundreds of individual vineyards are described as premier cru or grand cru in the classic wine regions of Alsace, Bordeaux, Burgundy and Champagne. The common denominator is that the wine can be counted on to be enormously expensive. On humbler wines, the use of the word cru tends to be mere decoration.

cru classé – See Classed growth.

cuve – A vat for wine, French.

cuvée – French for the wine in a *cuve*, or vat. The word is much used on labels to imply that the wine is from just one vat, and thus of unique, unblended character. Premier cuvée is supposedly the best wine from a given pressing because the grapes have had only the initial, gentle squashing to extract the free-run juice. Subsequent cuvées will have been from harsher pressings, grinding the grape pulp to extract the last drop of juice.

D

Dão – Major wine-producing region of northern Portugal now turning out much more interesting reds than it used to. Worth looking out for anything made by mega-producer Sogrape.

demi sec – 'Half-dry' style of French (and some other) wines. Beware. It can mean anything from off-dry to cloyingly sweet.

DO – Denominacion de Origen, Spain's wine-regulating scheme, similar to France's AC, but older – the first DO region was Rioja, from 1926. DO wines are Spain's best, accounting for a third of the nation's annual production.

DOC – Stands for Denominazione di Origine Controllata, Italy's equivalent of France's AC. The wines are made according to the stipulations of each of its 280 denominated zones of origin, 20 of which enjoy the superior classification of DOCG (DOC with *e Garantita* – 'guaranteed' – appended).

Durif – Rare black grape variety mostly of California, where it is also known as Petite Sirah, but with some plantings in Australia.

E

earthy – A tricky word in the wine vocabulary. In this book, its use is meant to be complimentary. It indicates that the wine somehow suggests the soil the grapes were grown in, even (perhaps a shade too poetically) the landscape in which the vineyards lie. The amazing-value red wines of the torrid, volcanic southernmost regions of Italy are often described as earthy. This is an association with the pleasantly 'scorched' back-flavour in wines made from the ultra-ripe harvests of this near-sub-tropical part of the world.

edge – A wine with edge is one with evident (although not excessive) acidity.

élevé – 'Brought up' in French. Much used on wine labels where the wine has been matured (brought up) in oak barrels – 'élevé en fûts de chêne' – to give it extra dimensions.

Entre Deux Mers – Meaning 'between two seas', it's a region lying between the Dordogne and Garonne rivers of Bordeaux, now mainly known for dry white wines from Sauvignon and Semillon grapes. Quality rarely seems exciting.

Estremadura – Wine-producing region occupying Portugal's coastal area north of Lisbon. Lots of interesting wines from indigenous grape varieties, usually at bargain prices. If a label mentions Estremadura, it is a safe rule that there might be something good within.

F

Faugères – AC of the Languedoc in south-west France. Source of many hearty, economic reds.

Feteasca – White grape variety widely grown in Romania. Name means 'maiden's grape' and the wine tends to be soft and slightly sweet.

Fiano – White grape variety of Sicily, lately revived. It is said to have been cultivated by the ancient Romans for a wine called Apianum.

finish – The last flavour lingering in the mouth after wine has been swallowed.

fino – Pale and very dry style of sherry. You drink it thoroughly chilled – and you don't keep it any longer after opening than other dry white wines. Needs to be fresh to be at its best.

Fitou – One of the first 'designer' wines, it's an appellation in France's Languedoc region, where production is dominated by one huge co-operative, the Vignerons de Mont Tauch. Back in the 1970s, this co-op paid a corporate-image company to come up with a Fitou logo and label-design style, and the wines have prospered ever since. And it's not just packaging – Fitou at all price levels can be very good value, especially from the Mont Tauch co-op.

flabby – Fun word describing a wine that tastes dilute or watery, with insufficient acidity.

flying winemaker – Back-labels on supermarket wines sometimes boast that the contents are made by a flying winemaker. They're consultants who visit vineyards worldwide at harvest time to oversee the production process, perhaps to ensure that the style of wine wanted by a major customer (usually a supermarket) is adhered to by the locals. These people are very often Australian, with degrees in oenology (the science of winemaking) and well up on the latest technology and biochemistry. If there is a criticism of flying winemakers, it is that they have a tendency to impose a uniform style on all the vineyards upon which they descend. Thus, more and more French, Italian and Spanish wines, for example, are starting to take on the 'upfront fruitiness' of the wines of Australia.

fruit – In tasting terms, the fruit is the greater part of the overall flavour of a wine. The wine is (or should be), after all, composed entirely of fruit.

G

Gamay – The black grape that makes all red Beaujolais. It is a pretty safe rule to avoid Gamay wines from any other region. It's a grape that does not do well elsewhere.

Garganega – White grape variety of the Veneto region of north-west Italy. Best known as the principal ingredient of Soave, but occasionally included in varietal blends and mentioned as such on labels. Correctly pronounced 'gar-GAN-iga'.

Garnacha – Spanish black grape variety synonymous with Grenache of France. It is blended with Tempranillo to make the red wines of Rioja and Navarra, and is now quite widely cultivated elsewhere in Spain to make grippingly fruity varietals.

garrigue – Arid land of France's deep south giving its name to a style of red wine that notionally evokes the herby, heated, peppery flavours associated with such a landscape. A tricky metaphor!

Gavi – DOCG for dry but rich white wine from Cortese grapes in Piedmont, north-east Italy. Trendy Gavi di Gavi wines tend to be enjoyably lush, but are rather expensive.

Gewürztraminer – One of the great grape varieties of Alsace, France. At their best, the wines are perfumed with lychees and are richly, spicily fruity, yet quite dry. Gewürztraminer from Alsace is almost always expensive – never under £5 – but the grape is also grown with some success in Eastern Europe, Germany, Italy and South America, and sold at more approachable prices. Pronounced 'geh-VOORTS-traminner'.

Givry – AC for red and white wines in the Côte Chalonnaise sub-region of Burgundy. Source of some wonderfully natural-tasting reds that might be lighter than those of more prestigious Côte d'Or to the north, but have great merits of their own. Relatively, the wines are often underpriced.

Graciano – Black grape variety of Spain that is one of the minor constituents of Rioja. Better known in its own right in Australia where it can make dense, spicy, long-lived red wines.

green – In flavour, a wine that is unripe and raw-tasting.

Grenache – The mainstay of the wines of the southern Rhône Valley in France. Grenache is usually the greater part of the mix in Côtes du Rhône reds and is widely planted right across the neighbouring Languedoc-Roussillon region. It's a big-cropping variety that thrives even in the hottest climates and is really a blending grape – most commonly with Syrah, the noble variety of the northern Rhône. Few French wines are labelled with its name, but the grape has caught on in Australia in a big way and it is now becoming a familiar varietal, known for strong, dark liquorous reds. Grenache is the French name for what is originally a Spanish variety, Garnacha.

Grillo – White grape of Sicily said to be among the island's oldest indigenous varieties, pre-dating the arrival of the Greeks in 600 BC. Much used for fortified Marsala, it has lately been revived for interesting, aromatic dry table wines.

grip – In wine-tasting terminology, the sensation in the mouth produced by a wine that has a healthy quantity of tannin in it. A wine with grip is a good wine. A wine with too much tannin, or which is still too young (the tannin hasn't 'softened' with age) is not described as having grip, but as mouth-puckering – or simply undrinkable.

Grüner Veltliner – The 'national' white-wine grape of Austria. In the past it made mostly soft, German-style everyday wines, but now is behind some excellent dry styles, too.

H

halbtrocken – 'Half-dry' in Germany's wine vocabulary. A reassurance that the wine is not some ghastly sugared Liebfraumilch-style confection.

hock – The wine of Germany's Rhine river valleys. It comes in brown bottles, as distinct from the wine of the Mosel river valleys – which comes in green ones.

I

Indicazione Geografica Tipica – Italy's recently instituted wine-quality designation, broadly equivalent to France's vin de pays. The label has to state the geographical location of the vineyard and will often (but not always) state the principal grape varieties from which the wine is made.

Inycon – A recent wine brand of Sicily's huge Settesoli co-operative and the label on several wines mentioned in this book. Inycon was the Ancient Greek name of the modern Sicilian village of Menfi where the vineyards and winery for the brand have been established.

J

jammy – The 'sweetness' in dry red wines is supposed to evoke ripeness rather than sugariness. Sometimes, flavours include a sweetness reminiscent of jam. Usually a fault in the winemaking technique.

joven – Young wine, Spanish. In regions such as Rioja, 'vino joven' is a synonym for *sin crianza*, which means 'without ageing' in cask or bottle.

K

Kabinett – Under Germany's bewildering wine-quality rules, this is a classification of a top-quality (QmP) wine. Expect a keen, dry, racy style. The name comes from the cabinet or cupboard in which winemakers traditionally kept their most treasured bottles.

Kekfrankos – Black grape variety of Hungary, particularly the Sopron region, which makes some of the country's more interesting red wines, characterised by colour and spiciness. Same variety as Austria's Blaufrankisch.

L

Lambrusco – The name is that of a black grape variety widely grown across northern Italy. True Lambrusco wine is red, dry and very slightly sparkling, but from the 1980s Britain has been deluged with a strange, sweet manifestation of the style, which has done little to enhance the good name of the original. Good Lambrusco is delicious and fun.

Languedoc-Roussillon – Vast area of southern France, including the country's south-west Mediterranean region. The source, now, of many great-value wines from countless ACs and vin de pays zones.

legs – The liquid residue left clinging to the sides of the glass after wine has been swirled. The persistence of the legs is an indicator of the weight of alcohol. Also known as 'tears'.

lieu dit – This is starting to appear on French wine labels. It translates as an 'agreed place' and is an area of vineyard defined as of particular character or merit, but not classified under wine law. Usually, the lieu dit's name is stated, with the implication that the wine in question has special value.

liquorice – The pungent, slightly burnt flavours of this once-fashionable confection are detectable in some wines made from very ripe grapes, for example the Malbec harvested in Argentina and several varieties grown in the very hot vineyards of southernmost Italy. A close synonym is 'tarry'. This characteristic is by no means a fault in red wine, unless very dominant, but it can make for a challenging flavour that might not appeal to all tastes.

liquorous – Wines of great weight and glyceriney texture (evidenced by the 'legs', or 'tears', which cling to the glass after the wine has been swirled) are always noteworthy. The connection with liquor is drawn in respect of the feel of the wine in the mouth, rather than with the higher alcoholic strength of spirits.

Lugana – DOC of Lombardy, Italy, known for a dry white wine that is often of real distinction – rich, almondy stuff from the ubiquitous Trebbiano grape.

M

Macabeo – One of the main grapes used for cava, the sparkling wine of Spain. It is the same grape as Viura.

Mâcon – Town and collective appellation of southern Burgundy, France. Lightweight white wines from Chardonnay grapes and similarly light reds from Pinot Noir and some Gamay. The better ones, and the ones exported, have the AC Mâcon-Villages and there are individual-village wines with their own ACs including Mâcon-Clessé, Mâcon-Viré and Mâcon-Lugny.

Malbec – Black grape variety grown on a small scale in Bordeaux, and the mainstay of the wines of Cahors in France's Dordogne region under the name Cot. Now much better known for producing big butch reds in Argentina.

Mantinia – Winemaking region of the Peloponnese, Greece. Dry whites from Moschofilero grapes are aromatic and refreshing.

Manzanilla – Pale, very dry sherry of Sanlucar de Barrameida, a grungy seaport on the southernmost coast of Spain. Manzanilla is proud to be distinct from the pale, very dry fino sherry of the main producing town of Jerez de la Frontera down the coast. Drink it chilled and fresh – it goes downhill in an opened bottle after just a few days, even if kept (as it should be) in the fridge.

Margaret River – Vineyard region of Western Australia regarded as ideal for grape varieties including Cabernet Sauvignon. It has a relatively cool climate and a reputation for making sophisticated wines, both red and white.

Marlborough – Best-known vineyard region of New Zealand's South Island has a cool climate and a name for brisk but cerebral Sauvignon Blanc and Chardonnay wines.

Marsanne – White grape variety of the northern Rhône Valley and, increasingly, of the wider south of France. It's known for making well-coloured wines with heady aroma and fruit.

Mataro – Black grape variety of Australia. It's the same as the Mourvèdre of France and Monastrell of Spain.

McLaren Vale – Vineyard region south of Adelaide in south-east Australia. Known for serious-quality wines from grape varieties including Shiraz and Chardonnay.

meaty – Weighty, rich red wine style.

Mendoza – The region to watch in Argentina. Lying to the east of the Andes mountains, just about opposite the best vineyards of Chile on the other side, Mendoza accounts for the bulk of Argentine wine production, with quality improving fast.

Merlot – One of the great black wine grapes of Bordeaux, and now grown all over the world. The name is said to derive from the French *merle*, meaning a blackbird. Characteristics of Merlot-based wines attract descriptions such as 'plummy' and 'plump' with black-cherry aroma. The grapes are larger than most, and thus have less skin in proportion to their flesh. This means the resulting wines have less tannin than wines from smaller-berry varieties such as Cabernet Sauvignon, and are therefore, in the Bordeaux context at least, more suitable for drinking while still relatively young.

middle palate – In wine-tasting, the impression given by the wine when it is held in the mouth.

Midi – Catch-all term for the deep south of France west of the Rhône Valley.

mineral – Good dry white wines can have a crispness and freshness that somehow evokes this word. Purity of flavour is a key.

Minervois – AC for (mostly) red wines from vineyards around the town of Minerve in the Languedoc-Roussillon region of France. Often good value. The new Minervois La Livinière AC – a sort of Minervois Grand Cru – is host to some great estates including Château Maris and Vignobles Lorgeril.

Monastrell – Black grape variety of Spain, widely planted in Mediterranean regions for inexpensive wines notable for their high alcohol and toughness – though they can mature into excellent, soft reds. The variety is known in France as Mourvèdre and in Australia as Mataro.

Monbazillac – AC for sweet, dessert wines within the wider appellation of Bergerac in south-west France. Made from the same grape varieties (principally Sauvignon and Semillon) that go into the much costlier counterpart wines of Barsac and Sauternes near Bordeaux, these stickies from botrytis-affected, late-harvested grapes can be delicious and good value for money.

Montalcino – Hill town of Tuscany, Italy, and a DOCG for strong and very long-lived red wines from Brunello grapes. The wines are mostly very expensive. Rosso di Montalcino, a DOC for the humbler wines of the zone, is often a good buy.

Montepulciano – Black grape variety of Italy. Best-known in Montepulciano d'Abruzzo, the juicy, purply-black and bramble-fruited red of the Abruzzi region mid-way down Italy's Adriatic side. Also the grape in the rightly popular hearty reds of Rosso Conero from around Ancona in the Marches. Not to be confused with the hill town of Montepulciano in Tuscany, famous for expensive Vino Nobile di Montepulciano wine.

morello – Lots of red wines have smells and flavours redolent of cherries. Morello cherries, among the darkest-coloured and sweetest of all varieties and the preferred choice of cherry-brandy producers, have a distinct sweetness resembled by some wines made from Merlot grapes. A morello whiff or taste is generally very welcome.

Moscatel – Spanish Muscat.

Moscato – See Muscat.

Moselle – The wine of Germany's Mosel river valleys, collectively known for winemaking purposes as Mosel-Saar-Ruwer. The wine always comes in slim, green bottles, as distinct from the brown bottles employed for Rhine wines.

Mourvèdre – Widely planted black grape variety of southern France. It's an ingredient in many of the wines of Provence, the Rhône and Languedoc, including the ubiquitous Vin de Pays d'Oc. It's a hot-climate vine and the wine is usually blended with other varieties to give sweet aromas and 'backbone' to the mix. Known as Mataro in Australia and Monastrell in Spain.

Muscadet – One of France's most familiar everyday whites. It comes from vineyards at the estuarial end of the river Loire, and at its best has something of a sea-breezy freshness about it. The better wines are reckoned to be those from the vineyards in the Sèvre et Maine region, and many are made *sur lie* – 'on the lees' – meaning that the wine is left in contact with the yeasty deposit of its fermentation until just before bottling, in an endeavour to add interest to what can sometimes be an acidic and fruitless style.

Muscat – Grape variety with origins in ancient Greece, and still grown widely among the Aegean islands for the production of sweet white wines. Muscats are the wines that taste more like grape juice than any other – but the high sugar levels ensure they are also among the most alcoholic of wines, too. Known as Moscato in Italy, the grape is much used for making sweet sparkling wines, as in Asti Spumante or Moscato d'Asti. There are several appellations in south-west France for inexpensive Muscats made rather like port, part-fermented before the addition of grape alcohol to halt the conversion of sugar into alcohol, creating a sweet and heady 'vin doux naturel'. Dry Muscat wines, when well made, have a delicious sweet aroma but a refreshing, light touch with flavours reminiscent variously of orange blossom, wood smoke and grapefruit.

must – New-pressed grape juice prior to fermentation.

N

Navarra – DO wine-producing region of northern Spain adjacent to, and overshadowed by, Rioja. Navarra's wines can be startlingly akin to their neighbouring rivals, and sometimes rather better value for money.

négociant – In France, a dealer-producer who buys wines from growers and matures and/or blends them for sale under his own label. Purists can be a bit sniffy about these entrepreneurs, claiming that only the vine-grower with his or her own winemaking set-up can make truly authentic stuff, but the truth is that many of the best wines of France are négociant-produced – especially at the humbler end of the price scale. Négociants are often identified on wine labels as 'négociant-éleveur' (literally 'dealer-bringer-up'), meaning that the wine has been matured, blended and bottled by the party in question.

Negro Amaro – Black grape variety mainly of Apulia, the fast-improving wine region of south-east Italy. Dense, earthy red wines with ageing potential and plenty of alcohol. The grape behind Copertino.

Nero d'Avola – Black grape variety of Sicily and southern Italy. It makes deep-coloured wines that, given half a chance, can develop intensity and richness with age.

non-vintage (NV) – A wine is described as such when it has been blended from the harvests of more than one year. No date is nominated on the label. A non-vintage wine is not necessarily an inferior one, but under quality-control regulations around the world, still table wines most usually derive solely from one year's grape crop to qualify for appellation status. Champagnes and sparkling wines are mostly blended from several vintages, as are fortified wines, such as basic port and sherry.

nose – In the vocabulary of the wine-taster, the nose is the scent of a wine. Sounds a bit dotty, but it makes a sensible enough alternative to the rather bald 'smell'. The use of the word 'perfume' implies that the wine smells particularly good. 'Aroma' is used specifically to describe a wine that smells as it should, as in 'this Burgundy has the authentic strawberry-raspberry aroma of Pinot Noir'.

O

oak – Most of the world's most expensive wines are matured in new or nearly new oak barrels, giving additional opulence of flavour. Of late, many cheaper wines have been getting the oak treatment, too, in older, cheaper casks, or simply by having sacks of oak chippings poured into their steel or fibreglass holding tanks. 'Oak aged' on a label is likely to indicate the latter treatments. But the overtly oaked wines of Australia have in some cases been so overdone, there is now a reactive trend whereby some producers proclaim their wines – particularly Chardonnays – as 'unoaked' on the label, thereby asserting that the flavours are more naturally achieved.

Oltrepo Pavese – Wine-producing zone of Piedmont, north-west Italy. The name means 'south of Pavia across the [river] Po' and the wines, both white and red, can be excellent quality and value for money.

organic wine – As in other sectors of the food industry, demand for organically made wine is – or appears to be – growing. As a rule, a wine qualifies as organic if it comes entirely from grapes grown in vineyards cultivated without the use of synthetic materials, and made in a winery where chemical treatments or additives are shunned with similar vigour. In fact, there are plenty of winemakers in the world using organic methods, but who disdain to label their bottles as such. Wines that do brazenly proclaim their organic status tend to carry the same sort of premium as their counterparts round the corner in the fruit, vegetable and meat aisles. The upshot is that there is only a limited choice of lower-priced organic wine. There is no single worldwide (or even Europe-wide) standard for organic food or wine, so you pretty much have to take the producer's word for it.

P

Pasqua – One of the biggest and, it should be said, best wine producers of the Veneto region of north-west Italy.

Passetoutgrains – Bourgogne passetoutgrains is a generic appellation of the Burgundy region, France. The word loosely means 'any grapes allowed' and is supposed specifically to designate a red wine made with Gamay grapes as well as Burgundy's principal black variety, Pinot Noir, in a ratio of two parts Gamay to one of Pinot. The wine is usually relatively inexpensive, and relatively uninteresting, too.

Periquita – Black grape variety of southern Portugal. Makes rather exotic spicy reds. Name means 'parrot'.

Petite Sirah – Black grape variety of California and Latin America known for plenty of colour and long life. Not related to the Syrah of the Rhône.

Petit Verdot – Black grape variety of Bordeaux used to give additional colour, density and spiciness to Cabernet Sauvignon-dominated blends. Strictly a minority player at home, but in Australia and California it is grown as the principal variety for some big hearty reds of real character.

petrol – When white wines from certain grapes, especially Riesling, are allowed to age in the bottle for longer than a year or two, they can take on a spirity aroma reminiscent of petrol or diesel. In grand mature German wines, this is considered a very good thing.

Picpoul – Obscure grape variety of southern France. Best known in Picpoul de Pinet, a weighty-ish dry white from near Carcassonne in the Languedoc. The name Picpoul means 'stings the lips' – referring to the natural high acidity of the juice.

Piemonte – North-western province of Italy, which we call Piedmont, known for the spumante wines of the town of Asti, plus expensive Barbaresco and Barolo and better-value varietal red wines from Barbera and Dolcetto grapes.

Pinotage – South Africa's own black grape variety. Makes red wines ranging from light and juicy to dark, strong and long-lived. It's a cross between Pinot Noir and a grape the South Africans used to call Hermitage (thus the portmanteau name) but turns out to have been Cinsault. Cheaper Pinotages tend to disappoint, but there has been an improvement of late in the standard of some wines tasted.

Pinot Blanc – White grape variety principally of Alsace, France. Florally perfumed, exotically fruity dry white wines.

Pinot Grigio – White grape variety of northern Italy. Wines bearing its name have become fashionable in recent times. Good examples have an interesting smoky-pungent aroma and keen, slaking fruit. But most are dull. Originally a French grape, there known as Pinot Gris, which is renowned for making lushly exotic – and expensive – white wines in the Alsace region.

Pinot Noir – The great black grape of Burgundy, France. It makes all the region's fabulously expensive red wines. Notoriously difficult to grow in warmer climates, it is nevertheless cultivated by countless intrepid winemakers in the New World intent on reproducing the magic appeal of red Burgundy. California and New Zealand have come closest, but rarely at prices much below those for the real thing. Some Chilean Pinot Noirs (Cono Sur, for example) are inexpensive and worth trying.

Pouilly Fuissé – Village and AC of the Mâconnais region of southern Burgundy in France. Dry white wines from Chardonnay grapes. Wines are among the highest-rated of the Mâconnais.

Pouilly Fumé – Village and AC of the Loire Valley in France. Dry white wines from Sauvignon Blanc grapes. Similar 'pebbly', 'grassy' or even 'gooseberry' style to neighbouring AC Sancerre. The notion put about by some enthusiasts that Pouilly Fumé is 'smoky' is surely nothing more than word-association with the name.

Primitivo – Black grape variety of southern Italy, especially the region of Apulia/Puglia. The wines are typically dense and dark in colour with plenty of alcohol, and have an earthy, spicy style. Often a real bargain. It is believed to be closely related to California's Zinfandel, which makes purple, brambly wines of a very different hue.

Prosecco – White grape variety of Italy's Veneto region which gives its name to a light, sparkling and cheap wine that is much appreciated locally, but not widely exported.

Puglia – The region occupying the 'heel' of southern Italy, and one of the world's fastest-improving sources of inexpensive wines. Modern winemaking techniques and large regional grants from the EU are at least partly responsible.

Q

QbA – German, standing for *Qualitätswein bestimmter Anbaugebiet*. It means 'quality wine from designated areas' and implies that the wine is made from grapes with a minimum level of ripeness, but it's by no means a guarantee of exciting quality. Only wines labelled QmP (see next entry) can be depended upon to be special.

QmP – Stands for *Qualitätswein mit Prädikat*. These are the serious wines of Germany, made without the addition of sugar to 'improve' them. To qualify for QmP status, the grapes must reach a level of ripeness as measured on a sweetness scale – all according to Germany's fiendishly complicated wine-quality regulations. Wines from grapes that reach the stated minimum level of sweetness qualify for the description of Kabinett. The next level up earns the rank of Spätlese, meaning 'late-picked'. Kabinett wines can be expected to be dry and brisk in style, and Spätlese wines a little bit riper and fuller. The next grade up, Auslese, meaning 'selected harvest', indicates a wine made from super-ripe grapes; it will be golden in colour and honeyed in flavour. A generation ago, these wines were as valued, and as expensive, as any of the world's grandest appellations, but the collapse in demand for German wines in the UK – brought about by the disrepute rightly earned for floods of filthy Liebfraumilch – means they are now seriously undervalued.

Quincy – AC of Loire Valley, France, known for pebbly-dry white wines from Sauvignon grapes. The wines are forever compared to those of nearby and much better-known Sancerre – and Quincy often represents better value for money. Pronounced 'KAN-see'.

Quinta – Portuguese for farm or estate. It precedes the names of many of Portugal's best-known wines. It is pronounced 'KEEN-ta'.

R

racy – Evocative wine-tasting description for wine that thrills the tastebuds with a rush of exciting sensations. Good Rieslings often qualify.

raisiny – Wines from grapes that have been very ripe or overripe at harvest can take on a smell and flavour akin to the concentrated, heat-dried sweetness of raisins. As a minor element in the character of a wine, this can add to the appeal but as a dominant characteristic it is a fault.

rancio – Spanish term harking back to Roman times when wines were commonly stored in jars outside, exposed to the sun, so they oxidised and took on a burnt sort of flavour. Today, rancio describes a baked – and by no means unpleasant – flavour in fortified wines, particularly sherry and Madeira.

Reserva – In Portugal and Spain, this has genuine significance. The Portuguese use it for special wines with a higher alcohol level and longer ageing, although the precise periods vary between regions. In Spain, especially in the Navarra and Rioja regions, it means the wine must have had at least a year in oak and two in bottle before release.

reserve – On French (as réserve) or other wines, this implies special-quality, longer-aged wines, but has no official significance.

Retsina – The universal white wine of Greece. It has been traditionally made in Attica, the region of Athens, for a very long time, and is said to owe its origins and name to the ancient custom of sealing amphorae (terracotta jars) of the wine with a gum made from pine resin. Some of the flavour of the resin inevitably transmitted itself into the wine, and ancient Greeks acquired a lasting taste for it.

Reuilly – AC of Loire Valley, France, for crisp dry whites from Sauvignon grapes. Pronounced 'RUR-yee'.

Ribatejo – Emerging wine region of Portugal. Worth seeking out on labels of red wines in particular, because new winemakers are producing lively stuff from distinctive indigenous grapes such as Castelao and Trincadeira.

Ribera del Duero – Classic wine region of north-west Spain lying along the river Duero (which crosses the border to become Portugal's Douro, forming the valley where port comes from). It is the home to an estate rather oddly named Vega Sicilia, where red wines of epic quality are made and sold at equally epic prices. Further down the scale, some very good reds are made, too.

Riesling – The noble grape variety of Germany. It is correctly pronounced 'REEZ-ling', not 'RICE-ling'. Once notorious as the grape behind all those boring 'medium' Liebfraumilches and Niersteiners, this grape has had a bad press. In fact, there has never been much, if any, Riesling in Germany's cheap-and-nasty plonks. But the country's best wines, the so-called Qualitätswein mit Prädikat grades, are made almost exclusively with Riesling. These wines range from crisply fresh and appley styles to extravagantly fruity, honeyed wines from late-harvested grapes. Excellent Riesling wines are also made in Alsace and now in Australia.

Rioja – The principal fine-wine region of Spain, in the country's north east. The pricier wines are noted for their vanilla-pod richness from long ageing in oak casks. Younger wines, labelled variously *joven* (young) and *sin-crianza* (meaning they are without barrel-ageing), are cheaper and can make relishable drinking.

Ripasso – A particular style of Valpolicella wine. New wine is partially refermented in vats that have been used to make the recioto reds (wines made from semi-dried grapes), thus creating a bigger, smoother (and more alcoholic) version of usually light and pale Valpolicella.

Riserva – In Italy, a wine made only in the best vintages, and allowed longer ageing in cask and bottle.

Rivaner – Alternative name for Germany's Müller Thurgau grape, the lifeblood of Liebfraumilch.

Riverland – Vineyard region to the immediate north of the Barossa Valley of South Australia, extending east into New South Wales.

Roditis – White grape variety of Greece, known for fresh dry whites with decent acidity, often included in the blend for retsina.

rosso – Red wine, Italy.

Rosso Conero – DOC red wine made in the environs of Ancona in the Marches, Italy. Made from the Montepulciano grape, the wine can provide excellent value for money.

Ruby Cabernet – Black grape variety of California, created by crossing Cabernet Sauvignon and Carignan. Makes soft and squelchy red wine at home and in South Africa.

Rueda – DO of north-west Spain making first-class refreshing dry whites from the indigenous Verdejo grape, imported Sauvignon grape, and others. Exciting quality – and prices, so far, are keen.

Rully – AC of Chalonnais region of southern Burgundy, France. White wines from Chardonnay and red wines from Pinot Noir grapes. Both can be very good and are substantially cheaper than their more northerly Burgundian neighbours. Pronounced 'ROO-yee'.

S

Saint Emilion – AC of Bordeaux, France. Centred on the romantic hill town of St Emilion, this famous sub-region makes some of the grandest red wines of France, but also some of the best-value ones. Less fashionable than the Médoc region on the opposite (west) bank of the river Gironde that bisects Bordeaux, St Emilion wines are made largely with the Merlot grape, and are relatively quick to mature. Each vintage since 1998 has produced many good wines – and some poor ones, too, it must be said – and most of the bottles to be found in supermarkets will be mature enough to drink now. The grandest wines are classified 1er Grand Cru Classé and are madly expensive, but many more are classified respectively Grand Cru Classé and Grand Cru, and these designations can be seen as a fairly trustworthy indicator of quality. There are several 'satellite' St Emilion ACs named after the villages at their centres, notably Lussac St Emilion, Montagne St Emilion and Puisseguin St Emilion. Some excellent wines are made by estates within these ACs, and at relatively affordable prices thanks to the comparatively humble status of their satellite designations.

Salento – Up and coming wine region of southern Italy. Many good bargain reds from local grapes including Nero d'Avola and Primitivo.

Sancerre – AC of the Loire Valley, France, renowned for flinty-fresh Sauvignon whites and rarer Pinot Noir reds. These wines are never cheap, and recent tastings make it plain that only the best-made, individual-producer wines are worth the money. Budget brands seem mostly dull.

Sangiovese – The local black grape of Tuscany, Italy. It is the principal variety used for Chianti and is now widely planted in Latin America – often making delicious, Chianti-like wines with characteristic cherryish-but-deeply-ripe fruit and a dry, clean finish. Chianti wines have become (unjustifiably) expensive in recent years and cheaper Italian wines such as those called Sangiovese di Toscana make a consoling substitute.

Santorini – Island of Greece's Cyclades was the site in about 1500 BC of a tremendous volcanic explosion. The huge caldera of the volcano – a circular mini-archipelago – is now planted with vines producing very trendy and likeable dry white wines at fair prices.

Saumur – Town and appellation of Loire Valley, France. Characterful minerally red wines from Cabernet Franc grapes, and some whites. The once-popular sparkling wines from Chenin Blanc grapes are now little seen in Britain.

Saumur-Champigny – Separate appellation for red wines from Cabernet Franc grapes of Saumur in the Loire, sometimes very good and lively.

Sauvignon Blanc – French white grape variety now grown worldwide. New Zealand is successfully challenging the long supremacy of French ACs such as Sancerre. The wines are characterised by aromas of gooseberry, fresh-cut grass, even asparagus. Flavours are often described as 'grassy' or 'nettley'.

sec – Dry wine style. French.

secco – Dry wine style. Italian.

Semillon – White grape variety originally of Bordeaux, where it is blended with Sauvignon Blanc to make fresh dry whites and, when harvested very late in the season, the ambrosial sweet whites of Barsac, Sauternes and other appellations. Even in the driest wines, the grape can be recognised from its honeyed, sweet-pineapple, even banana-like aromas. Now widely planted in Australia and Latin America, and frequently blended with Chardonnay to make dry whites, some of them interesting.

sherry – The great aperitif wine of Spain, centred on the Andalusian city of Jerez (from which the name 'sherry' is an English mispronunciation). There is a lot of sherry-style wine in the world, but only the authentic wine from Jerez and the neighbouring producing towns of Puerta de Santa Maria and Sanlucar de Barrameida may label their wines as such. The Spanish drink real sherry: very dry and fresh, pale in colour and served well chilled, called fino and manzanilla; and darker but naturally dry variations called amontillado, palo cortado and oloroso. The stuff sold under the big brand names for the British market is sweetened, coloured commercial yuck for putting in trifles or sideboard decanters to gather dust. The sherries recommended in this book are all real wines, made the way the Spanish like them.

Shiraz – Australian name for the Syrah grape. The variety is the most widely planted of any in Australia, and makes red wines of wildly varying quality, characterised by dense colour, high alcohol, spicy fruit and generous, cushiony texture.

Sogrape – The leading wine company of Portugal, which built its fortune on Mateus Rosé. Sogrape is based in the Douro region, where port comes from, and makes many excellent table wines both locally and further afield. In 2002, Sogrape added the huge port (and sherry) house of Sandeman to its port-making interests.

Somontano – Wine region of north-east Spain. Name means 'under the mountains' – in this case the Pyrenees – and the region has had DO status only since 1984. Much innovative winemaking here, with New World styles emerging. Some very good buys. A region to watch.

souple – French wine-tasting term that translates into English as 'supple' or even 'docile', as in 'pliable', but I understand it in the vinous context to mean muscular but soft – a wine with tannin as well as soft fruit.

Spätlese – See QmP.

spirity – Some wines, mostly from the New World, are made from grapes so ripe at harvest that their high alcohol content can be detected through a mildly burning sensation on the tongue, similar to the effect of sipping a spirit.

spritzy – Describes a wine with a barely detectable sparkle. Some young wines are intended to have this elusive fizziness; in others it is a fault.

spumante – Sparkling wine of Italy. Asti Spumante is the best known, from the town of Asti in the north-west Italian province of Piemonte. The term describes wines that are fully sparkling. Frizzante wines have a less vigorous mousse.

stalky – A useful tasting term to describe red wines with flavours that make you think the stalks from the grape bunches must have been fermented along with the must (juice). Young Bordeaux reds very often have this mild astringency. In moderation it's fine, but if it dominates it probably signifies the wine is at best immature and at worst badly made.

Stellenbosch – Town and region at the heart of South Africa's burgeoning wine industry. It's an hour's drive from Cape Town and the source of much of the country's cheaper wine. Quality is variable, and the name Stellenbosch on a label can't (yet, anyway) be taken as a guarantee of quality.

stony – Wine-tasting term for keenly dry white wines. It's meant to indicate a wine of purity and real quality, with just the right match of fruit and acidity.

structured – Good wines are not one-dimensional; they have layers of flavour and texture. A structured wine has phases of enjoyment: the 'attack' or first impression in the mouth; the middle palate as the wine is held in the mouth; the lingering aftertaste.

summer fruit – Wine-tasting term intended to convey a smell or taste of soft fruits such as strawberries and raspberries – without having to commit too specifically to which.

Superiore – On labels of Italian wines, this is more than an idle boast. Under DOC rules, wines must qualify for the superiore designation by reaching one or more specified quality levels, usually a higher alcohol content or an additional period of maturation. Frascati, for example, qualifies for DOC status at 11.5 per cent alcohol, but to be classified superiore must have 12 per cent alcohol.

sur lie – Literally, 'on the lees'. It's a term now widely used on the labels of Muscadet wines, signifying that after fermentation has died down, the new wine has been left in the tank over the winter on the lees – the detritus of yeasts and other interesting compounds left over from the turbid fermentation process. The idea is that additional interest is imparted into the flavour of the wine.

Syrah – The noble grape of the Rhône Valley, France. Makes very dark, dense wine characterised by peppery, tarry aromas. Now planted all over southern France and farther afield. In Australia, where it makes wines ranging from disagreeably jam-like plonks to wonderfully rich and silky keeping wines, it is known as Shiraz.

T

table wine – Wine that is unfortified and of an alcoholic strength, for UK tax purposes anyway, of no more than 15 per cent. I use the term to distinguish, for example, between the red table wines of the Douro Valley in Portugal and the region's better-known fortified wine, port.

Tafelwein – Table wine, German. The humblest quality designation, which doesn't usually bode very well.

tank method – Bulk-production process for sparkling wines. Base wine undergoes secondary fermentation in a large, sealed vat rather than in individual closed bottles. Also known as the Charmat method after the name of the inventor of the process.

tannin – Well known as the film-forming, teeth-coating component in tea, tannin is a natural compound occurring in black grape skins and acts as a natural preservative in wine. Its noticeable presence in wine is regarded as a good thing. It gives young everyday reds their dryness, firmness of flavour and backbone. And it helps high-quality reds to retain their lively fruitiness for many years. A grand Bordeaux red when first made, for example, will have purply-sweet, rich fruit and mouth-puckering tannin, but after ten years or so this will have evolved into a delectably fruity mature wine in which the formerly parching effects of the tannin have receded almost completely, leaving the shade of 'residual tannin' that marks out a great wine approaching maturity.

Tarrango – Black grape variety of Australia.

tarry – On the whole, winemakers don't like critics to say their wines evoke the redolence of road repairs, but I can't help using this term to describe the agreeable, sweet, 'burnt' flavour that is often found at the centre of the fruit in wines from Argentina, Italy and Portugal in particular.

TCA – Dread ailment in wine caused by faulty corks. It stands for 2,4,6-trichloroanisol and is characterised by a horrible musty smell and flavour in the affected wine. It is largely because of the current plague of TCA that so many wine producers worldwide are now going over to polymer 'corks' and screwcaps.

tears The colourless alcohol in the wine left clinging to the inside of the glass after the contents have been swirled. Persistent tears (also known as 'legs') indicate a wine of good concentration.

Tempranillo – The great black grape of Spain. Along with Garnacha (Grenache in France) it makes all red Rioja and Navarra wines and, under many pseudonyms, is an important or exclusive contributor to the wines of many other regions of Spain. It is also widely cultivated in South America.

tinto – On Spanish labels indicates a deeply coloured red wine. 'Clarete' denotes a paler colour. Also Portuguese.

Toro – Quality wine region east of Zamora, Spain.

Torrontes – White grape variety of Argentina. Makes soft, dry wines, often with delicious grapey-spicy aroma, similar in style to the classic dry Muscat wines of Alsace, but at more accessible prices.

Touraine – Region encompassing a swathe of the Loire Valley, France. Non-AC wines may be labelled 'Sauvignon de Touraine' etc.

Touriga Nacional – The most valued black grape variety of the Douro Valley in Portugal, where port is made. The name Touriga now appears on an increasing number of table wines made as sidelines by the port producers. They can be very good, with the same spirity aroma and sleek flavours of port itself, minus the fortification.

Traminer – Grape variety, the same as Gewürztraminer.

Trebbiano – The workhorse white grape of Italy. A productive variety that is easy to cultivate, it seems to be included in just about every ordinary white wine of the entire nation – including Frascati, Orvieto and Soave. It is the same grape as France's Ugni Blanc. There are, however, distinct regional variations of the grape. Trebbiano di Lugana makes a distinctive white in the DOC of the name, sometimes very good, while Trebbiano di Toscana makes a major contribution to the distinctly less interesting dry whites of Chianti country.

Trincadeira Preta – Portuguese black grape variety native to the port-producing vineyards of the Douro Valley (where it goes under the name Tinta Amarella). In southern Portugal, it produces dark and sturdy table wines.

trocken – 'Dry' German wine. It's a recent trend among commercial-scale producers in the Rhine and Mosel to label their wines with this description in the hope of reassuring consumers that the contents do not resemble the dreaded sugar-water Liebfraumilch-type plonks of the bad old days. But the description does have a particular meaning under German wine law, namely that there is only a low level of unfermented sugar lingering in the wine (nine grams per litre, if you need to know), and this can leave the wine tasting rather austere.

U

Ugni Blanc – The most widely cultivated white grape variety of France and the mainstay of many a cheap dry white wine. To date it has been better known as the provider of base wine for distilling into Armagnac and Cognac, but lately the name has been appearing on wine labels. Technology seems to be improving the performance of the grape. The curious name is pronounced 'OON-yee', and is the same variety as Italy's ubiquitous Trebbiano.

V

Vacqueyras – Village of the southern Rhône valley of France in the region better known for its generic appellation, the Côtes du Rhône. Vacqueyras can date its winemaking history all the way back to 1414, but has only been producing under its own village AC since 1991. The wines, from Grenache and Syrah grapes, can be wonderfully silky and intense, spicy and long-lived.

Valdepeñas – An island of quality production amidst the ocean of mediocrity that is Spain's La Mancha region – where most of the grapes are grown for distilling into the head-banging brandies of Jerez. Valdepeñas reds are made from a grape they call the Cencibel – which turns out to be a very close relation of the Tempranillo grape that is the mainstay of the fine but expensive red wines of Rioja. Again, like Rioja, Valdepeñas wines are matured in oak casks to give them a vanilla-rich smoothness. Among bargain reds, Valdepeñas is a name to look out for.

Valpolicella – Red wine of Verona, Italy. Good examples have ripe, cherry fruit and a pleasingly dry finish. Unfortunately, there are many bad examples of Valpolicella. Shop with circumspection. Valpolicella Classico wines, from the best vineyards clustered around the town, are more reliable. Those additionally labelled superiore have higher alcohol and some bottle-age.

vanilla – Ageing wines in oak barrels (or, less picturesquely, adding oak chips to wine in huge concrete vats) imparts a range of characteristics including a smell of vanilla from the ethyl vanilline naturally given off by oak.

varietal – A varietal wine is one named after the grape variety (one or more) from which it is made. Nearly all everyday wines worldwide are now labelled in this way. It is salutary to contemplate that just 20 years ago, wines described thus were virtually unknown outside Germany and one or two quirky regions of France and Italy.

vegan-friendly – My informal way of noting that a wine is claimed to have been made not only with animal-product-free finings (see Vegetarian wine) but without any animal-related products whatsoever, such as manure in the vineyards.

vegetal – A tasting note definitely open to interpretation. It suggests a smell or flavour reminiscent less of fruit (apple, pineapple, strawberry and the like) than of something leafy or even root-based. Some wines are evocative (to some tastes) of beetroot, cabbage or even unlikelier vegetable flavours – and these characteristics may add materially to the attraction of the wine.

vegetarian wine – Given that proper wine consists of nothing other than grape juice and the occasional innocent natural additive, it might seem facile to qualify it as a vegetable product. But most wines are 'fined' – clarified – with animal products. These include egg whites, isinglass from fish bladders and casein from milk. Gelatin, a beef by-product briefly banned by the UK government at the hysterical height of the BSE scare, is also used. Consumers who prefer to avoid contact, however remote, with these products, should look out for wines labelled as suitable for vegetarians and/or vegans. The wines will have been fined with bentonite, an absorbent clay first found at Benton in the US state of Montana.

Verdejo – White grape of the Rueda region in north-west Spain. It can make superbly perfumed crisp dry whites of truly distinctive character and has helped make Rueda one of the best white-wine sources of Europe. No relation to Verdelho.

Verdelho – Portuguese grape variety once mainly used for a medium-dry style of Madeira, also called Verdelho, but now rare. The vine is now prospering in Australia, where it can make well-balanced dry whites with fleeting richness and lemon-lime acidity.

Verdicchio – White grape variety of Italy best known in the DOC zone of Castelli dei Jesi in the Adriatic wine region of the Marches. Dry white wines once known for little more than their naff amphora-style bottles but now gaining a reputation for interesting, herbaceous flavours of recognisable character.

Vermentino – White grape variety principally of Italy, especially Sardinia. Makes florally scented soft dry whites.

Vieilles vignes – Old vines. Many French producers like to claim on their labels that the wine within is from vines of notable antiquity. While it's true that vines don't produce useful grapes for the first few years after planting, it is uncertain whether vines of much greater age – say 25 years plus – than others actually make better fruit. There are no regulations governing the use of the term, so it's not a reliable indicator anyway.

Vin Délimité de Qualité Supérieur – Usually abbreviated to VDQS, a French wine-quality designation between appellation contrôlée and vin de pays. To qualify, the wine has to be from approved grape varieties grown in a defined zone. This designation is gradually disappearing.

vin de liqueur – Sweet style of white wine mostly from the Pyrenean region of south-westernmost France, made by adding a little spirit to the new wine before it has fermented out, halting the fermentation and retaining sugar.

vin de pays – 'Country wine' of France. The French map is divided up into more than 100 vin de pays regions. Wine in bottles labelled as such must be from grapes grown in the nominated zone or département. Some vin de pays areas are huge: the Vin de Pays d'Oc (named after the Languedoc region) covers much of the Midi and Provence. Plenty of wines bearing this humble designation are of astoundingly high quality and certainly compete with New World counterparts for interest and value.

Vin de Pays Catalan – Zone of sub-Pyrenees region (Roussillon) of south-west France.

Vin de Pays de L'Hérault – Zone within Languedoc-Roussillon region of south-west France.

Vin de Pays des Coteaux du Luberon – Zone of Provence, France.

Vin de Pays des Côtes de Gascogne – Zone of 'Gascony' region in south-west France.

Vin de Pays de Vaucluse – Zone of southern Rhône Valley.

Vin de Pays d'Oc – Largest of the zones, encompasses much of the huge region of the Languedoc of south-west France. Many excellent wines are sold under this classification, particularly those made in appellation areas from grapes not permitted locally.

Vin de Pays du Gers – Zone of south-west France including Gascony. White wines principally from Ugni Blanc and Colombard grapes.

Vin de Pays du Jardin de la France – Zone of the Loire Valley.

vin de table – The humblest official classification of French wine. Neither the region, grape varieties nor vintage need to be stated on the label. The wine might not even be French. Don't expect too much from this kind of 'table wine'.

vin doux – Sweet, mildly fortified wine mostly of France, usually labelled 'vin doux naturel'. A little spirit is added during the winemaking process, halting the fermentation by killing the yeast before it has consumed all the sugars – thus the pronounced sweetness of the wine.

vin gris – Rosé wine from Provence. They call it gris ('grey') because it's halfway between red (the new black, you might say) and white.

Vinho de mesa – 'Table wine' of Portugal.

Vino da tavola – The humblest official classification of Italian wine. Much ordinary plonk bears this designation, but the bizarre quirks of Italy's wine laws dictate that some of that country's finest wines are also classed as mere vino da tavola (table wine). If an expensive Italian wine is labelled as such, it doesn't mean it will be a disappointment.

Vino de mesa – 'Table wine' of Spain. Usually very ordinary.

vintage – The grape harvest. The year displayed on bottle labels is the year of the harvest. Wines bearing no date have been blended from the harvests of two or more years.

Viognier – A grape variety once exclusive to the northern Rhône Valley in France where it makes a very chi-chi wine, Condrieu, usually costing £20 plus. Now, the Viognier is grown more widely, in North and South America as well as elsewhere in France, and occasionally produces soft, marrowy whites that echo the grand style of Condrieu itself.

Viura – White grape variety of Rioja, Spain. Also widely grown elsewhere in Spain under the name Macabeo. Wines have a blossomy aroma and are dry, but sometimes soft at the expense of acidity.

Vouvray – AC of the Loire Valley, France, known for still and sparkling dry white wines and sweet, still whites from late-harvested grapes. The wines, all from Chenin Blanc grapes, have a unique capacity for unctuous softness combined with lively freshness – an effect best portrayed in the demi-sec (slightly sweet) wines, which can be delicious and keenly priced. Unfashionable, but worth looking out for.

W

weight – In an ideal world the weight of a wine is determined by the ripeness of the grapes from which it has been made. In some cases the weight is determined merely by the quantity of sugar added during the production process. A good, genuine wine described as having weight is one in which there is plenty of alcohol and 'extract' – colour and flavour from the grapes. Wine enthusiasts judge weight by swirling the wine in the glass and then examining the 'legs' or 'tears' left clinging to the inside of the glass after the contents have subsided. Alcohol gives these runlets a dense, glycerine-like condition, and if they cling for a long time, the wine is deemed to have weight – a very good thing in all honestly made wines.

Winzergenossenschaft – One of the many very lengthy and peculiar words regularly found on labels of German wines.

This means a winemaking co-operative. Many excellent German wines are made by these associations of growers.

woodsap – A subjective tasting note. Some wines have a fleeting bitterness, which is not a fault, but an interesting balancing factor amidst very ripe flavours. The effect somehow evokes woodsap.

X

Xarel-lo – One of the main grape varieties for cava, the sparkling wine of Spain.

Xinomavro – Black grape variety of Greece. It retains its acidity even in the very hot conditions that prevail in many Greek vineyards – where harvests tend to overripen and make cooked-tasting wines. Modern winemaking techniques are capable of making well-balanced wines from Xinomavro.

Y

Yecla – Town and DO wine region of eastern Spain, close to Alicante, making lots of interesting, strong-flavoured red and white wines, often at bargain prices.

yellow – White wines are not white at all, but various shades of yellow – or, more poetically, gold. Some white wines with opulent richness even have a flavour I cannot resist calling yellow – reminiscent of butter.

Z

Zefir – Hungarian white grape variety that can (on a good day) produce a spicy, dry wine rather like the Gewürztraminer of Alsace.

Zenit – Hungarian white grape variety. Produces dry wines.

Zinfandel – Black grape variety of California. Makes brambly reds, some of which can age very gracefully, and 'blush' whites – actually pink, because a little of the skin colour is allowed to leach into the must. The vine is also planted in Australia and South America. The Primitivo of southern Italy is said to be a related variety, but makes a very different kind of wine.

——Wine Rituals——

There has always been a lot of nonsense talked about the correct ways to serve wine. Red wine, we are told, should be opened and allowed to 'breathe' before pouring. White wine should be chilled. Wine doesn't go with soup, tomatoes or chocolate. You know the sort of thing.

It would all be simply laughable except that these daft conventions do make so many potential wine lovers nervous about the simple ritual of opening a bottle and sharing it around. Here is a short and opinionated guide to the received wisdom.

Breathing

Simply uncorking a wine for an hour or two before you serve it will make absolutely no difference to the way it tastes. However, if you wish to warm up an icy bottle of red by placing it near (never on) a radiator or fire, do remove the cork first. As the wine warms, even very slightly, it gives off gas, which will spoil the flavour if it cannot escape.

Chambré-ing

One of the more florid terms in the wine vocabulary. The idea is that red wine should be at the same temperature as the room (chambre) you're going to drink it in. In fairness, it makes sense – although the term harks back to the days when the only people who drank wine were those who could afford to keep it in the freezing cold vaulted cellars beneath their houses. The ridiculously high temperatures to which some homes are raised by central heating systems today are really far too warm for wine. But presumably those who live in such circumstances do so out of choice, and will prefer their wine to be similarly overheated.

Chilling

Drink your white wine as cold as you like. It's certainly true that good whites are at their best at a cool rather than at an icy temperature, but cheap and characterless wines can be improved immeasurably if they are cold enough – the anaesthetising effect of the temperature removes all sense of taste. Pay no attention to notions that red wine should not be served cool. There are plenty of lightweight reds that will respond very well to an hour in the fridge.

Corked wine

Wine trade surveys reveal that far too many bottles are in no fit state to be sold. The villain is very often cited as the cork. Cut from the bark of cork-oak trees cultivated for the purpose in Portugal and Spain, these natural stoppers have done sterling service for 200 years, but now face a crisis of confidence among wine producers. A diseased or damaged cork can make the wine taste stale because air has penetrated, or musty-mushroomy due to a chemical reaction. These faults in wine, known as 'corked' or 'corky', should be immediately obvious, even in the humblest bottle, so you should return the bottle to the supplier and demand a refund. A warning here. Bad corks tend to come in batches. It might be wise not to accept another bottle of the same wine, but to choose something else.

Today, more and more wine producers are opting to close their bottles with polymer bungs. Some are designed to resemble the 'real thing' while others come in a rather disorienting range of colours – including black. There seems to be no evidence that these synthetic products do any harm to the wine, but it might not be sensible to 'lay down' bottles closed with polymer. The effects of years of contact with these materials are yet to be scientifically established.

Corkscrews

The best kind of corkscrew is the 'waiter's friend' type. It looks like a pen-knife, unfolding a 'worm' (the helix or screw) and a lever device which, after the worm has been driven into the cork (try to centre it) rests on the lip of the bottle and enables you to withdraw the cork with minimal effort. These devices are cheaper and longer-lasting than any of the more elaborate types, and are equally effective at withdrawing polymer bungs – which can be hellishly difficult to unwind from Teflon-coated 'continuous' corkscrews like the Screwpull.

Decanting

There are two views on the merits of decanting wines. The prevailing one seems to be that it is pointless and even pretentious. The other is that it can make real improvements in the way a wine tastes and is definitely worth the trouble.

Of course, it's all too easy to drift into the dangerous realms of pretentiousness here, but there's nothing like a real experiment to keep minds concentrated on the facts. Scientists, not usually much exercised by the finer nuances of wine, will tell you that exposure to the air causes wine to 'oxidise' – take in oxygen molecules that will quite quickly initiate the process of turning wine into vinegar – and anyone who has tasted a 'morning-after' glass of wine will no doubt vouch for this.

But the fact that wine does oxidise is a genuine clue to the reality of the effects of exposure to air. Shut inside its bottle, a young wine is very much a live substance, jumping with natural, but mysterious, compounds that can cause all sorts of strange taste sensations. But by exposing the wine to air these effects are markedly reduced.

In wines that spend longer in the bottle, the influence of these factors diminishes, in a process called 'reduction'. In red wines, the hardness of tannin – the natural preservative imparted into wine from the grape skins – gradually reduces, just as the raw purple colour darkens to ruby and later to orangey-brown.

I believe there is less reason for decanting old wines than new, unless the old wine has thrown a deposit and needs carefully to be poured off it. And in some light-bodied wines, such as older Rioja, decanting is probably a bad idea because it can accelerate oxidation all too quickly.

As to actual experiments, I have carried out several of my own, with wines opened in advance or wines decanted compared to the same wines just opened and poured, and my own unscientific judgement is that big, young, alcoholic reds can certainly be improved by aeration. So I was pleased to read about two distinguished doctors who carried out a revealing experiment of their own in the hope of proving once and for all whether there is any point in opening a bottle of red wine in advance.

Dr Nirmal Charan is a pulmonologist (lung specialist) of Boise, Idaho, USA. Dr Pier Giuseppe Agostoni is a cardiologist from the University of Milan in Italy. Their experiment was intended to resolve a good-natured disagreement that arose between them over the dinner table at Dr Charan's home in Idaho. The host suggested to Dr Agostoni that he might like to try a bottle of Idaho wine. Dr A assented but suggested to Dr C it would be a good idea to open the bottle an hour or so in advance to let it breathe.

As a consultant in pulmonary medicine and something of an expert in matters of respiration, Dr C pointed out to his guest that there was no scientific basis for the suggested course of action. In the proper spirit of empiricism, the two agreed that the dispute should be settled by a controlled test.

And so the following day the learned pair adjourned to Dr C's laboratory at the VA Medical Center in Boise, armed with five bottles of Cabernet Sauvignon. The cork of each bottle was penetrated with a hypodermic needle and a small sample of wine taken. Each was measured for oxygen pressure in an arterial blood gas analyser, giving the reading of 30 ml of mercury (as compared to 90 ml in well-oxygenated human blood).

Next, the wines were opened. Further samples were taken after periods of two, four, six and 24 hours. For the first periods, the reading remained unaltered. Only after 24 hours had it increased significantly – to 61 ml.

Meanwhile, the doctors tried pouring samples from another bottle of the wine into glasses and swirling it round. After only a couple of minutes, the reading reached 150.

Dr Agostoni was impressed. He returned to Milan and put his new-found wisdom to the test by inviting 35 friends to a party. He gave them all wine that had been swirled, and then wine that had been newly opened. Only two among the throng acknowledged no difference.

Then Dr A gave the guests a 'blind' tasting of swirled and unswirled wines. To his considerable satisfaction, all but one were able to tell the difference, and agreed the wine tasted significantly better with aeration.

Dr A passed these results on to his friend back in Idaho. The grateful Dr Charan was able to incorporate the information into a sideshow presentation at that year's meeting of the American Lung Association in Chicago. 'Just like blood,' Dr C told an enthralled audience of pulmonologists and thoracic surgeons, 'oxygenated wine is better than non-oxygenated wine.'

Glasses

Does it make any difference whether you drink your wine from a hand-blown crystal glass or a plastic cup? Do experiment! Conventional wisdom suggests that the ideal glass is clear, uncut, long-stemmed and with a tulip-shaped bowl large enough to hold a generous quantity when filled only half-way up. The idea is that you can hold the glass by its stalk rather than by its bowl. This gives an uninterrupted view of the colour, and prevents you smearing the bowl with your sticky fingers. By filling the glass only half-way up, you give the wine a chance to 'bloom', showing off its wonderful perfume. You can then intrude your nose into the air space within the glass, without getting it wet, to savour the bouquet. It's all harmless fun, really – and quite difficult to perform if the glass is an undersized Paris goblet filled, like a pub measure, to the brim.

Washing glasses

If your wine glasses are of any value to you, don't put them in the dishwasher. Over time, they'll craze from the heat of the water. And they will not emerge in the glitteringly pristine condition suggested by the pictures on some detergent packets. For genuinely perfect glasses that will stay that way, wash them in hot soapy water, rinse with clean, hot water and dry immediately with a glass cloth kept exclusively for this purpose. Sounds like fanaticism, but if you take your wine seriously, you'll see there is sense in it.

Keeping wine

How long can you keep an opened bottle of wine before it goes downhill? Not long. A re-corked bottle with just a glassful out of it should stay fresh until the day after, but if there is a lot of air inside the bottle, the wine will oxidise, turning progressively stale and sour. Wine 'saving' devices that allow you to withdraw the air from the bottle via a punctured, self-sealing rubber stopper are variably effective, but don't expect these to keep a wine fresh for more than a couple of re-openings. A crafty method of keeping a half-finished bottle is to decant it, via a funnel, into a clean half bottle and recork.

Storing wine

Supermarket labels always seem to advise that 'this wine should be consumed within one year of purchase'. I think this is a wheeze to persuade customers to drink it up quickly and come back for more. Many of the more robust red wines are likely to stay in good condition for much more than one year, and plenty will actually improve with age. On the other hand, it is a sensible axiom that inexpensive dry white wines are better the younger they are. If you do intend to store wines for longer than a few weeks, do pay heed to the conventional wisdom that bottles are best stored in low, stable temperatures, preferably in the dark. Bottles closed with conventional corks should be laid on their side lest the corks dry out for lack of contact with the wine. But one of the notable advantages of the new closures now proliferating is that if your wine comes with a polymer 'cork' or a screwcap, you can safely store it upright.

——Wine and Food——

Wine is made to be drunk with food, but some wines go better with particular dishes than others. It is no coincidence that Italian wines, characterised by soft, cherry fruit and a clean, mouth-drying finish, go so well with the sticky delights of pasta.

But it's personal taste rather than national associations that should determine the choice of wine with food. And if you prefer a black-hearted Argentinian Malbec to a brambly Italian Barbera with your Bolognese, that's fine.

The conventions that have grown up around wine and food pairings do make some sense, just the same. I was thrilled to learn in the early days of my drinking career that sweet, dessert wines can go well with strong blue cheese. As I don't much like puddings, but love sweet wines, I was eager to test this match – and I'm here to tell you that it works very well indeed as the end-piece to a grand meal in which there is cheese as well as pud on offer.

Red wine and cheese are supposed to be a natural match, but I'm not so sure. Reds can taste awfully tinny with soft cheeses such as Brie and Camembert, and even worse with goat's cheese. A really extravagant, yellow Australian Chardonnay will make a better match. Hard cheeses such as Cheddar and the wonderful Old Amsterdam (top-of-the-market Gouda) are better with reds.

And then there's the delicate issue of fish. Red wine is supposed to be a no-no. This might well be true of grilled and wholly unadorned white fish, such as sole or a delicate dish of prawns, scallops or crab. But what about oven-roasted monkfish or a substantial winter-season fish pie? An edgy red will do very well indeed, and provide much comfort for those many among us who simply prefer to drink red wine with food, and white wine on its own.

It is very often the method by which dishes are prepared, rather than their core ingredients, that determines which wine will work best. To be didactic, I would always choose Beaujolais or summer-fruit-style reds such as those from Pinot Noir grapes to go with a simple roast chicken. But if the bird is cooked as coq au vin with a hefty wine sauce, I would plump for a much more assertive red.

Some sauces, it is alleged, will overwhelm all wines. Salsa and curry come to mind. I have carried out a number of experiments into this great issue of our time, in my capacity as consultant to a company that specialises in supplying wines to Asian restaurants. One discovery I have made is that forcefully fruity dry white wines with keen acidity can go very well indeed even with fairly incendiary dishes. Sauvignon Blanc with Madras? Give it a try!

I'm also convinced, however, that some red wines will stand up very well to a bit of heat. The marvellously robust Argentinian reds that get such frequent mentions in this book are good partners to Mexican chilli-hot recipes and salsa dishes. The dry, tannic edge to these wines provides a good counterpoint to the inflammatory spices in the food.

Some foods are supposedly impossible to match with wine. Eggs and chocolate are among the prime offenders. And yet, legendary cook Elizabeth David's best-selling autobiography was entitled *An Omelette and a Glass of Wine*, and the affiliation between chocolates and Champagne is an unbreakable one. Taste is, after all, that most personally governed of all senses. If your choice is a boiled egg washed down with a glass of claret, who is to say otherwise?

Index